COL
CUL

EXAM
THE
CEN
IDE
CR

AGE
URE

NING
21ST
RY'S
ITY
SIS

LIVING IN THE MESS
BY MANDY KAHN

RULES FOR A COMPOSITION
BY BRIAN ROETTINGER

THE DEATH OF SUBCULTURE
BY AARON ROSE

jrp|ringier

Living In The Mess

P. 5–45

by Mandy Kahn

The PERFECT CIRCLES and DORIC LINES of the ancient world are buried at Pompeii, and anyway, flawless things make the people beside them more cracked and ragged. Better to show off the broken thing, the jarring thing, a mess of the purposely mismatched. At the very least it makes us feel like we're telling the truth.

* * *

Enough
time
in
the
randomness
and
patterns
make
themselves
apparent—
even
there,
in
the
place
from
which
order
was
banished.

I wasn't interested in patterns but there they suddenly were, and then they were everywhere, which made them invisible.

* * *

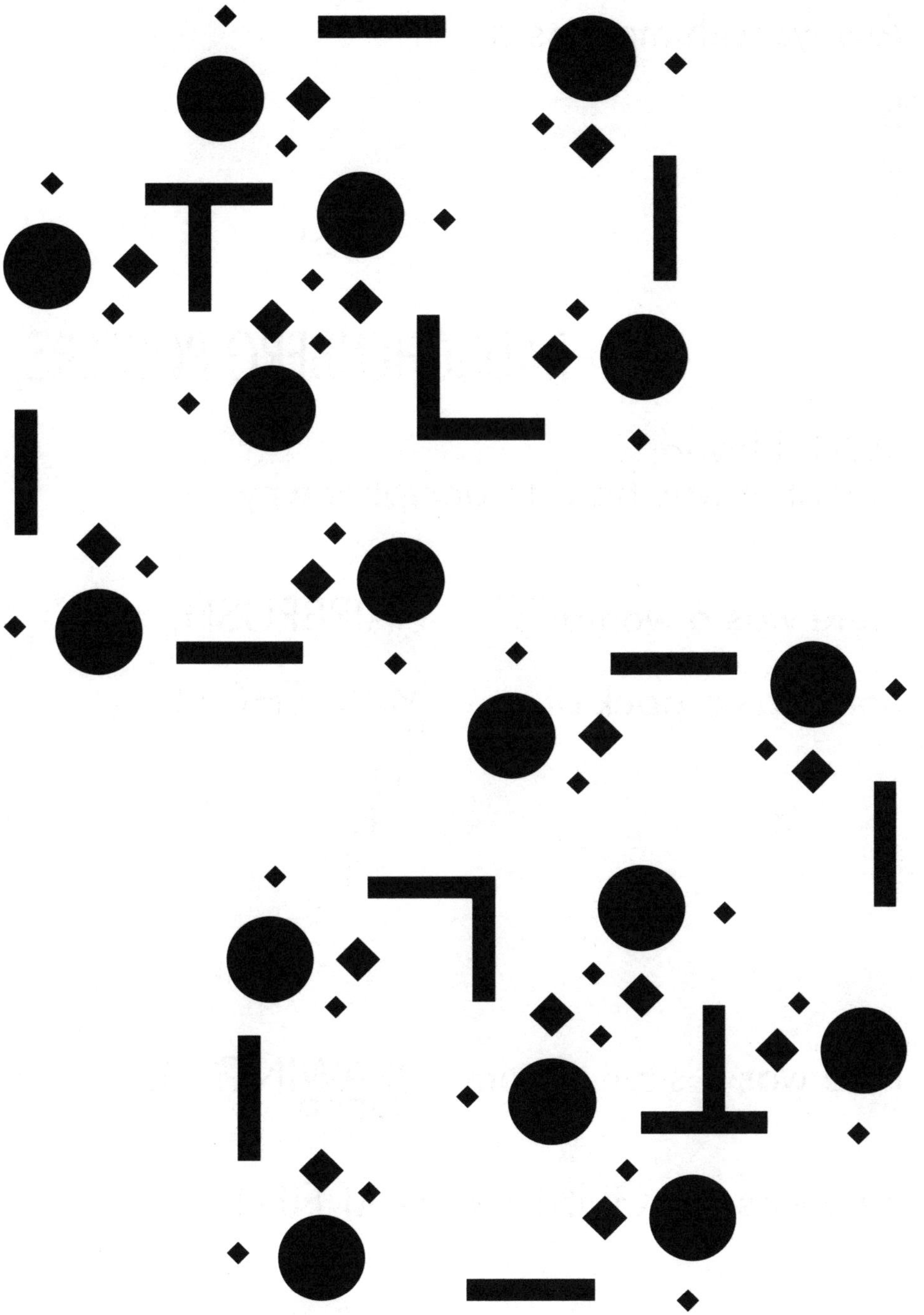

Always with me was a

b
o
o
k
of

RAUSCHENBERG POSTERS,

which I loved,
though it was hard to decipher why.

Here was a woman's HAIRBRUSH,

here was a pack of MARATHON
R
U
N
N
E
R
S,

here was a sitting room DRAWING OF
SHEEP,

here was A GUSTY WHEAT FIELD.

These cuttings,
seemingly
unrelated,
were
glued together
in
a
pattern I
found inexplicable—
if it
were a math
problem
I'd call
it
unsolvable—
and though
no part felt
inherently
beautiful I found
beauty in the
resulting
combination,
which
was maybe a
visual beauty
and
maybe
the dug-up
beauty of
an
idea.

LIKE EVERYONE ELSE

I spent the first decade of the new millennium making nests of cast-off things, of pieces culled from eras past I wove together without pattern—

my own hairbrush

and marathon runners

and line-drawn sheep

and windy clumps of wheat.

AND THEN ONE DAY I LOOKED AROUND AND SAID, I'M LIVING IN A RAUSCHENBERG POSTER, AND THE SONG THAT'S PLAYING IS A RAUSCHENBERG TOO, AND THE BOOK OF POEMS ON MY BEDSIDE TABLE, FOUND POEMS MADE FROM SCRAPS OF EXTANT MATERIAL, IS ONE ALSO—AND THAT'S WHEN I STARTED TO FEEL UNSETTLED.

* * *

Sometime during elementary school I saw a television program about motion sickness. This was of special interest to me as I've always been queasy on long drives, on whale-watching trips, in films with hand-held camerawork. We feel nauseous, the program explained, when our brain receives clashing messages—when the body says I'm bouncing furiously while the eyes say I'm on steady waters, for example. Some people are more sensitive to this discrepancy than others. I've always been unusually susceptible—embarrassingly delicate in travel, for example—the first in any boating party to turn green. And maybe that's why I started to feel in my gut the affects of discrepancy in the new millennium, as much as I loved the new millennium—as much as I wanted everything to be threadbare and disintegrated, as much as I chose to live in intentional discordance: still. I

wanted
to
choose
the
mess
and
became
increasingly
fearful
the
mess
had
chosen
me.

* * *

When Natalie Cole's iteration of the pop song "Unforgettable" became a considerable BILLBOARD HIT in 1991,

I THOUGHT IT WAS A CHEAT.

She hadn't even written the song, I argued—she'd done nothing more than add a vocal track to a song of her father's—she'd simply squeezed a hit out of a hit. Value, I argued, lay in original creation. The collage she'd made was a lower form of art—a trick—a deeply American show of, well, laziness and greed.

Years later I came to understand the genius in Natalie Cole's stroke. Her vocals added an entire dimension to a listener's experience, a dimension created by the relationship between the song's components. After all, her father, Nat "King" Cole, had passed away in '65. That added dimension was furnished to bursting with filial piety, a child's mourning, triumph over missing; the new version moved listeners to tears in a way the first never had. That extra dimension is the complex, layered province of collage: it's the tension, the depth, the feeling and meaning that comes from juxtaposition, and it's the realm, I later realized, I was pretty much living in.

* * *

I'd noticed Natalie Cole's turn in part because it was rare. But ten years later, songs made from the cut-up parts of other songs were so prevalent you'd be hard-pressed to notice. Or rather, you'd be hard-pressed to remember it hadn't always been that songs were made by sampling other songs. And anyhow, so much had changed since 1991 that the trend towards borrowing was barely a blip on the new screens that were everywhere—in our offices, in our pockets and purses, even imbedded in the backs of the plane seats in front of us—even in the dashboards of our cars.

• •

What could possibly be dangerous about borrowing from other times—times we knew inherently, times we collectively missed? What could be less dangerous than a pack of ardent runners, a hairbrush and a somehow-familiar sheep?

• •

By then I'd been a teacher and knew how hard it was to get students
to understand tone.

And that extra dimension a collage creates, the invisible but palpable and complex dimension, is a realm of tone entirely. <u>To make sense of a collage the viewer must guess with what tone its elements have been joined.</u>

But tone is subtle and an ear for it is hard for some to cultivate. Without such an ear, works of collage become N O I S E or U N F I X E D P U Z Z L E S .

The early 2000s saw a tone-important trend in the arrival of the

I
R
O
N
I
C M
O
U
S
T
A
C
H
E,

a
favorite
at
the
shows
I
was
then
frequenting.

The first group to wear it—a tiny number, a handful at best—joined it with a certain heavy smirk. The two—SMIRK and MOUSTACHE—were never seen apart, because without the smirk the moustache became its own grotesque opposite, its own photo in negative. The moustache itself was exceptionally shaggy—an exaggeration, if one was possible, of the version popular in the nineteen-eighties among television and porn actors. It was worn with neither reverence nor nostalgia, though some of our fathers and uncles had once displayed it with pride. This was not a way to align ourselves with our fathers and our uncles. It was a way to separate ourselves, because its tone, dictated by the smirk, was wholly inscrutable to many, and so to many the moustache was puzzling or repellant or taken as its opposite, a tribute. That moustache, on some level, became the locked door to a speakeasy many would neither locate nor have the credentials to enter.

For those who wore it, the ironic moustache was a stroke of ultimate brashness, a thing they knew was on the surface ugly but intended to make meaningful, even attractive, by marrying it to an idea. It was worn, said the smirk, to make you laugh, or guffaw, or as a conversation piece, or to indicate confidence: I can wear something ugly <u>on my face</u> and still be impossibly attractive. That smirk was a negative sign placed before the moustache itself, transforming the ugly to its opposite, but only for those who understood.

But as the moustache disseminated, the smirk it carried dissipated. The next wave of wearers, and certainly the next after those, may have only been able to explain the moustache by saying it was retro, it was cool. Once it was popular, it stopped being ugly and therefore stopped being funny. Without the smirk it was a plain, straight thing, worn for normal reasons.

Though their absolute value is the same, negative six and positive six are mathematical opposites. The negative sign tells us whether to plot a value on the number line towards the positive side or into the land of negatives. Tone, similarly, tells us where to plot a value. For example: If we ascribe a random number to the wearing of a college sweatshirt to demonstrate an earnest love of a school—let's say a positive six—then the wearing of that same sweatshirt to mock the college-loving becomes a negative six. Tone will let an onlooker know whether to plot that sweatshirt's value on the positive or negative side of zero on the number line, whether it's worn to mean the thing itself or its opposite. Tone is all-important, then—an absolute imperative for understanding, for the accurate communication of meaning. What happens when tone can't be determined by a viewer? In that case, the thing might be wrongly ascribed an opposite meaning to what had been intended—mathematically, negative six might be read as positive six. But even more often, things are left uncategorized—

I don't know what it means, it's confusing, I don't have time to figure it out—

and everything, whether meant to be positive or negative, becomes its absolute value—a number of paces to move without the map that says which way to go—the thing itself, but meaningless—a word, say, written in cuneiform—a symbol.

THERE IS DANGER IN A LANDSCAPE
OF MEANINGLESS SYMBOLS.

The first decade of the twenty-first century saw a record number of tone-important revivals—revival after revival, coming faster and faster, until they were piling up, happening concurrently, creating a kind of retro salad in which tone was drowned, meaning was forgotten, and things became only a parade of undesignated symbols, which is why

I loved this decade, and which is why it came to worry me.

* * *

HOW DIFFERENT IS THE IRONIC MOUSTACHE FROM MUCH OF CONCEPTUAL ART?

Each relies on the beauty of an idea to advance its project, and charts its course at times by way of ugliness. Faced with the conundrum of preference posed by poet Wallace Stevens, both conceptual art and moustache choose the latter:

I DO NOT KNOW WHICH TO PREFER, / THE BEAUTY OF INFLECTIONS / OR THE BEAUTY OF INNUENDOES, / THE BLACKBIRD WHISTLING / OR JUST AFTER.

* * *

I say "collage culture" because the cutting and pasting of extant things has replaced the act of original creation in the new millennium as the favored creative method. Musicians and artists, designers and writers, jewelry makers and interior decorators employ the method of collage—a method that once felt foreign and daring—with such incredible frequency now that nobody notices.

* * *

Sometimes the fashions of entire decades were revived, sometimes just pieces—the 50s prom dress became a rage, and 60s leather Beatle boots, 80s shoulder pads and 40s swimsuits. The past, it seemed, and increasingly, felt, was being ransacked: rummaged so its component parts could be joyfully cut from their contexts, joined with other things and assigned a different tone: in essence, collaged.

The New Year's Eve that welcomed the millennium was fraught with heavy fear. Computers weren't made to handle the date change, went common lore: they might all crash and New Year's Day devolve to temporary anarchy. People prepared for power outages, shortages of water. They pulled out large amounts of cash, should banking systems go. As the date transitioned there was an audible roar at the party I attended, as a roomful of revelers waited to s
e
e

whether the power would cut out.

IT DIDN'T.

Corporations had scrambled to fix computer GLITCHES ahead of time. And though anarchy didn't arrive when people feared it would, it did arrive, at least in boisterous spirit: Y2K had started a decade that looted the closets of history, that picked through the sounds and styles of the past like the strictures of time no longer applied, that borrowed and bore with a kind of electric frenzy—till it was harder and harder to tell by sight what year it was we were living in.

* * *

From London's *The Times*, July 2008:

"The fashion crimes of the 1970s have, it seems, been forgiven, or forgotten. Unbelievably, the maxi-dress and flared trousers are making a comeback. Last week I spotted someone in Bond Street wearing a tie-dyed poncho, without matching irony. In February there was the relaunch of Halston, the iconic 1970s label, at New York Fashion Week. And no one even sniggered."

From *The Toronto Star* (reporting on New York's Fashion Week), September 2008:

"The other look was one of cheery optimism: bright colour, joyful prints and the 60s…"

From London's *Daily Mail*, September 2008:

"Shorts—yes; disco glitter—certainly: neon pink—a must have. All of which add up to an obvious eighties revival…"

From Melbourne's *Sunday Age*, December 2007:

"Paisleys and flower prints spell a hippie revival—even if they are garish…"

From Glasgow's *Evening Times*, May 2009:

"The revival of 1940s-style glamour has created a craze for pin-curls, tea dresses, luscious red lipstick and seamed stockings."

From Brisbane and Queensland's *The Courier Mail*, November 2009, from an article on men's shorts:

"It's a bit of a 1980s-'90s feel but it could also be a revival of '30s menswear or '50s college style," she says."

From *Sydney Morning Herald*, August 2008:

"But Allen's biggest impact on fashion to date has been her championing of the 1950s-style prom dress... The 'prom' dress—with the help of some other big-name backers—is enjoying a fashion revival."

From *Sydney Morning Herald*, April 2008:

"We're no longer living in the seventies but it appears to be the decade that a lot of people most want to revisit. Once dismissed as the decade that taste forgot, there is now a growing demand for 1970s memorabilia, no matter how tacky. Supporting this revival is the second annual Living In The 70s Fair, to be held on Sunday, May 4 at the Susannah Place Museum in The Rocks in Sydney."

From Sydney's *The Sun Herald*, January 2008:

"Designers would have us dressed for a soiree at Jay Gatsby's mansion this summer, as the 1920s roar back to the runway. According to Women's Wear Daily, Karl Lagerfeld's models for Chanel's spring 2008 ready-to-wear shows in Paris and New York accessorised their crisp, sporty looks with tennis racquets, although they seemed more likely to indulge in a post-game gin and tonic than a sports drink. Drop-waist and flapper dresses also featured at J. Mendel, Nina Ricci, Moschino, Christian Dior and Anna Sui, while Chris Benz paired '20s-style slouchy pants with silk shirts and floppy hats."

From London's *The Sunday Times*, August 2009:

"Head for the peace of Sussex's South Downs, where you can step back in time and celebrate five decades of British popular culture. The event is Vintage 2010 and the buzz is the music, fashion and lifestyle of the 1940s, 50s, 60s, 70s and 80s, all on show in the fabulous grounds of the Goodwood estate…. This three-day festival will be a chance to dive into your favourite era. 'The idea is to create five zones, representing each decade….' There will also be contemporary musicians on hand, performing on the 'Inspired by' stage…. If you fancy learning the dance moves of your chosen era, there will be teachers on hand."

* * *

When
my
parents
divorced,
my
dad
retained
our
family
house.

Far into the nineties, it kept its seventies form: sunken living room, orange carpeting, drapes in an oversized floral pattern, giant mirrors, wallpaper in brown and tan. I loved that house, even when it fell from fashion; I remember a classmate saying

that
visiting
felt

like
entering

a
time
warp.

My mom's next house, designed in the eighties, was similarly a product of its era: walls in baby blue and mint, down-stuffed couches, pastel flowers, lace.

Those were decades when home-décor was carefully matched—not only in style and color and pattern, but also in era. My mother would never have let a mid-century love seat cross her eighties threshold. And my father, who knew nothing about design, would still have somehow known it was taboo to switch my mother's couch with his. These aesthetic rules were so entrenched that violating them would have made a person appear unhinged.

In July of 2008, The Sydney Morning Herald describes a home this way:

> The owner's collection of mid-century furniture includes original Barcelona chairs by Mies van der Rohe and Lilly Reich, and Arne Jacobsen's 1958 egg chair. These, together with an art collection that includes original works by Francis Bacon, set the tone for the new interior. "It combines with the classic architecture to create a mix of old and new that can be very stimulating," says Parr.

This is from an article titled "Sydney's (Best) Houses." The next home profiled features "an oriental coffee table and oversized black chinoiseries cupboard, French neoclassic Louis dining chairs, African sculptures, mid-century chairs." SUCH A MIX, IN THE PERFECT EIGHTIES, would have made its owner an oddball. Now anything is fair game for plundering and incorporation—any point of origin, any moment in time.

* * *

W	CAN'T	IS
H	GET	THE
A	OUT	CONCEPT
T	OF	OF
	MY	MOTION
I	MIND	SICKNESS.

When the body gets two dissimilar pieces of information—<u>I'm stationary</u> from the eyes and <u>I'm bouncing</u> from the body—we feel physical symptoms.

I speak to Johannes Burge, a post-doctoral researcher at the Center for Perceptual Systems in the Department of Psychology at the University of Texas at Austin.

I ask whether collage in fashion or interior design or music might affect the way one feels. If an outfit tells the brain, for example, THE YEAR IS NINETEEN-EIGHTY and the year is nineteen-fifty-five concurrently, or a room does, might that send the body into a sort of does-not-compute mode, resulting in a nausea similar to seasickness?

As far as he's aware, no one has ever tested for this. He's not entirely comfortable making leaps of faith, but he does say:

> Two cues about a single environmental property telling you different things equals feeling bad. Could the same sort of thing happen with collage? Well, I would stipulate this: If there is a collage of any sort where it dissociates two cues that are normally yoked then you're probably going to end up feeling bad, but my guess is that it would only work if those two cues normally tell you about the same environmental property. So in the case of seasickness you've got two cues, vision and the vestibular system, telling you about body orientation—if they're mismatched, you feel bad. If there's something which pops up in any of the thirteen different forms of collage that you're considering, then would that analogous relationship hold?—I suspect you're going to end up with some discomfort. If not, if it's just context, probably no discomfort, but if there's any sort of dissociation between two things that are normally yoked then there possibly would be.

* * *

Los Angeles harbors the means of creative production. Ideas that are born here are transmitted to the rest of the world with staggering speed—we have the movie cameras, the music studios, the concrete factories downtown ready to multiply a pair of pants by twenty thousand.

This city fuses wings onto our notions, so that before we've made up our minds entirely, they've flown from us.

I've been told no cultural movement starts in a single place, which I don't disbelieve.

The Internet serves as a kind of cosmic consciousness, conjoining us all, and it's silly to lay ownership to something as big as a trend.

That said,
it felt like we were
at the point of germination,
the place where the cell was splitting,
and there was giddiness to it,
a whiff of agency or power.

Someone decided to dress up for the party in something strange and then clothes were being manufactured, were being boxed and shipped, were on the bodies of high school freshmen who didn't know us. But the question remains: Why did we turn to the past? Those parties were full of art school students, filmmakers, musicians, graphic designers: creative minds of every possible stripe. Why didn't they invent a style so singular their fingerprint would be indelible? Wasn't there anything anyone wanted to say?

But borrowing was saying—it was bestowing favor, it was creating an in-crowd of those who could judge tone, it was expressing the abandon and rowdy spirit inherent in plundering. And so the revivals came faster and faster, till everything was being revived, it felt, at once—all moments in our collective past were alive again, concurrently, and suddenly we could pick and choose between them. The dance floor at the Vine Bar was alive with sixties fringe, eighties shoulder pads and thirties waistcoats.

And for the record, this had nothing to do with drugs—who needed them? The walls of time, for us, were already porous.

* * *

Before it arrived, I assumed the millennium would bring new trends in culture, immediately after burning the old trends down. I was wrong. It didn't burn—it looted.

I'd been trained by the former century, when every decade wanted to be new. Just as a mob at Comiskey Park burned disco records with audible glee, each decade of the twentieth century involved a thorough housecleaning and a methodical reinvention. Fifties strictures and rules of decorum were burned in the love fires of the sixties Haight, for example. The excesses of the twenties were denounced through the prudence of the thirties. Like teenagers, each generation labored to become itself, and defined itself in exact opposition to what had come before, as if the opposite aesthetic was by definition the most rebellious.

BUT
NOTHING
FEELS MORE
TIRED

THAN A PREDICTABLE REBELLION.

After a century of reinvention, perhaps nothing seemed more revolutionary than borrowing, using, valuing—than crediting the past, even worshipping it—and in doing so, throwing off the hampering need to invent.

When we'd tired of burning, we looted. And I suspect someday we'll burn our loot.

* * *

Better known as Girl Talk, Gregg Gillis is a mash-up artist; his craft lies in the manipulation of chunks of extant songs. His first album, Night Ripper, uses more than a hundred samples, and his follow-up Feed the Animals quotes upwards of three hundred. He's especially frenetic when playing live; egged on by an audience, he's been known to quote an album's worth of samples in a handful of minutes.

Notable is the incredible familiarity of the songs Gillis chooses to use: each one such a radio favorite its notes are etched in our collective history. The first time I heard Feed the Animals I felt I was on a children's ride through the halls of my own past, but on fast-forward—here was the song that brought everyone onto the dance floor at our sixth grade prom, here was the song my stepmother played ad nauseam on cassette—but as soon as a melody swam to the surface another one would clobber it. I was chasing every memory, but fruitlessly, exhaustively: sometimes getting gripping chunks but never getting wholes. Apparently a reporter at The Montreal Gazette had a similar experience: "The effect is as dizzying as it is intoxicating. You barely have time to react to one combination of associations before it is replaced by another, and another, and another." Which, as it turns out, is intentional. Gillis tells London's The Guardian, "I always wanted to use recognizable elements and play with people's emotional, nostalgic connections with these songs.... For me the biggest challenge is to make transformative new music out of these huge musical parts that anyone can recognize."

And so suddenly, not just parts of songs but parts of associated memories are being looped, sped, scratched and stacked together. What could be more hallucinatory? What could be more surreal?

Used to be that drugs, or hypnotism, or psychotherapy were required to plumb those depths.

Like a drug trip, however, we can't choose where we go. And like a drug trip, there's risk: what's accessed within us can be wonderful but it can also be sinister. The human brain buries things for reasons. A hypnotist approaches his work carefully; Gillis seems almost brash. "I like these songs to be familiar so you either love them or hate them, that they have some kind of memory I can manipulate," Gillis tells The Daily Telegraph.

I've seen Gillis play; no one gets people dancing faster. As he carries the crowd from sample to sample, between places we remember, all of us pressed together and dancing as hard as our bodies will go, there's a feeling of shared excitement, and it's intoxicating. There's a feeling that we're headed somewhere, and we're going there together, and good or bad, we're willing: we've signed on for the duration.

* * *

> That is the case with NEW08. When artists take found or ready-made objects heavily imbued with a nostalgic resonance—such as Argyle's record covers, Hinkley's newspaper or Bond's old paperbacks—and augment them drastically to make them speak their own thoughtful language, curious things begin to happen: the objects dislodge from their original identity and start to evoke new emotions and associations.

– Melbourne's *The Age*, in a review of an art opening at Australia's Center for Contemporary Art, March 2008

* * *

I ask Johannes Burge whether listeners can process the samples in a Girl Talk song at the pace they occur, even if their conscious minds can't keep up. He sends me an article from Nature Neuroscience that makes me think they can.

Our system processes visual data with seventy-five percent accuracy in fewer than thirty milliseconds, the article explains. And, says Johannes, auditory processing is faster:

> Now audition is much faster than vision. Audition is a much more reliable sense for temporal processing. I can't give you numbers on this but I can guess it can detect things down in the single digit millisecond range pretty easily.

But most of the processing done at this speed is subconscious. Researchers, when testing for visual perception, will flash an image on a screen for a slice of time—let's say thirty milliseconds—and ask a volunteer whether he saw anything. At that speed, he'll say he didn't. Then researchers will force him to choose between two possible images as the thing he saw. If seventy-five of a hundred volunteers choose the correct image, it is said we process visual data at thirty milliseconds with seventy-five percent accuracy.

But still, the volunteer will think he hasn't seen anything. Says Johannes,

> There's a lot of processing going on that people are only very faintly aware of. You can only get them to show you that they've been able to process the information—through careful experimentation—but they won't ever tell you that they were able to process it, quote unquote, consciously.

He calls the samples Girl Talk uses "jingles":

> If you put lots and lots of jingles into a very short period of time and ask [test subjects] to identify the jingles, they'll be able to get a few of them but not all of them. They probably will still have processed the ones they can't identify or even would swear to you aren't there.

When a song comes on the radio that stirs a particular memory, that memory has the chance to bloom in the conscious, to be pondered. We might spend the time it plays wistfully revisiting, turning over a moment or a feeling in the mind. The trouble with a Girl Talk song is the speed at which it happens—faster than the conscious mind but slow enough for the subconscious.

Gillis layers samples so we get old songs concurrently, and so memories, as quick as they come, are braided into rope—rubbed against each other for ferocity, for friction. We leave feeling elated or dazed or dumbed or shaken or raw, oblivious to the specifics of what we've undergone. Things happen to us but without us, because of their speed—they slip right past the part of us we think of as ourselves.

* * *

> It really depends on the class and the level of the students I get. Most of the time, however, my students would struggle with tone. They tend to be very literal and have a hard time getting irony and sarcasm. They tend to assume that whatever the author is saying is absolutely true.

–Ruoc Le, English and English Language teacher at Hawthorne High School

So I teach, as I said, four different periods of History, and if I show a movie in those four class periods there will be different responses even though they're all eighth graders. We have implicit tracking because the orchestra and band classes are only offered a couple of times a day and those kids are oftentimes in geometry and a little bit more advanced. So I'll watch a movie with the kids as we're doing the Civil War—if there's a joke in that movie, maybe the one class the kids will laugh and get it and in my other three classes it'll be totally silent. And having done this for a long time, I still can't figure out what it is, you know? It's very bizarre that all kids don't laugh at the joke.

—Jeff Schwartz, history teacher at Lincoln Middle School

* * *

IS ●●●●● THE ●●●●● MAJORITY BEING ●●●●● LEFT ●●●●● OUT OF ●●●●● THE JOKE, ●●●●● OR THE PATHOS, ●●●●● OR ●●●●● THE MEANING ●●●●● OF THINGS?

* * *

Maybe we tired of having everything. Maybe it stopped presenting a challenge. Hunting for the out-of-print loses its luster if everything's online. And maybe all this access became exhausting, or stifling.

In May of 2009, The Economist ran an article with the tag line, "Contemporary jewellery is more about ideas than the flaunting of wealth." It begins: "Through the centuries people have worn jewellery to depict status, wealth and identity. Now there is another reason." That other reason, according to the article, is to display an intellectual vigor, a playfulness, a penchant for the associations of contemporary art. "Pieces," it reads, "can be made of anything: found objects, recycled junk, textiles, plastic—even paper. If they include precious metals and gemstones, these rarely appear in conventional forms.... Humor and subversion are an intrinsic element of this kind of jewellery."

The late 2000s saw the meteoric rise of photographer Todd Selby, whose website features photos of the apartments of the highly creative—graphic designers, musicians and painters in New York and Paris and Los Angeles and Tokyo—messy lofts with new work sometimes scotch taped to the walls. These apartments are spread with tchotchkes and equipment, mismatched furniture and towers of books, crisscrossed by cords, hung with mobiles, littered with folded papers: they are lived-in, cluttered, imperfect and stunning, brightly-colored and utterly real, and they became a sensation overnight.

Mixed in among those pictured are rockstars and socialites and supermodels and heirs—those who have the means for building perfect spaces but opt instead to tack to walls the things they like in the fashion of the still-struggling. Like buyers of collaged jewelry, these people prize ideas over materials, and the wealthy play on an equal field with those of modest means—value lays in the picking, the cutting, the ordering, as if to say: Being able to purchase isn't interesting anymore. Creative prowess is the new wealth.

* * *

"It is the age of collage: of things cut out and cut up and copied and pasted, to craft an illusion that is somehow more real than the sum of its parts," writes a reporter for South Africa's The Weekender, as part of his 2009 review of an opening for artist Asha Zero. But Zero's art isn't collage—it's post-collage.

> Edgy, punky cut-ups, sliced & diced from magazines, newspapers, and the net, reassembled on canvas board with the crazy dedication of Dr. Frankenstein in his lab. But crazier: these aren't mixed-media collages after all, but painstakingly painted replications of paper collages, down to the last tear, rip and wrinkle…. All in acrylic, and all on board…. It is only when you set your gaze on macro that you can appreciate the photorealistic intensity of the technique, and even then, you may not believe your eyes.

* * *

Noticing takes time, plus a desire, plus an inclination, especially in a world where there is too much to see: To consider something deeply a dozen other things must be concertedly ignored.

Imagine a pair of girls working an assembly line at a bottling plant. When they interact, they miss a bottle, and once they've missed the first, all goes to bedlam; bottles pile up like something out of vaudeville. The machine is bigger—it chooses the pace. Trying to keep up turns into slapstick.

The twenty-first century is bigger and faster than we are. To consider a single bottle, we must be content to miss many others, which feels irresponsible: we've been trained to keep up. Concentration makes us different to the point of eccentricity.

AND SO I STARTED TO FEEL ECCENTRIC, AND TO APPEAR ECCENTRIC.

A friend said, I don't mind that you fail to answer my calls; when we're together, you ignore the calls of others and give me your complete attention. This approach has been hard to explain to my parents. My mother answers the telephone no matter when it rings. She is trying to keep up, bottle after bottle: if she misses one, she knows the conveyor belt won't pause.

I've taken to reading fiction from the American nineteen-fifties, that foreign place where living rooms match and

poem-lines are written from scratch,

not borrowed; where small things happen with heavy resonance because a person, if he is so inclined, has the time to interact with them, to determine their weight or decide to lend them such.

How strange COLLAGE ART must have seemed back then, how exciting, how beautiful, which is how the nineteen-fifties feel to me.

* * *

T
H
E

refrain of the
contemporary
world

s
e
e
m
s

to

b
e

<u>I didn't realize he meant it as a joke</u>

<u>He was being serious</u>

<u>She was actually mad</u>

<u>She meant it ironically—</u>

<u>I can't derive tone from an email.</u>

Emails are written quickly, so that parts of grammar are sacrificed, the parts of grammar that help determine how a message should be interpreted; and they're consumed quickly, so the time required to get their meaning is truncated.

We send and receive an incredible volume of correspondence, but what of it? Wouldn't a fraction of the number of messages, prepared and consumed with care, ultimately succeed at communicating more?

AREN'T WE JUST DECORATING
OUR SCREENS WITH MEANINGLESS
SYMBOLS, FILLING OUR TIME WITH
THE SCANNING OF THEM, AND
LOADING OUR CONVEYOR
B
E
L
T
WITH USELESS BOTTLES?

* * *

In 2007, The Washington Post's Gene Weingarten planted Joshua Bell, a violinist who sells out Lincoln Center, in the D.C. subway to play for tips.

> Each passerby had a quick choice to make, one familiar to commuters in any urban area where the occasional street performer is part of the cityscape: Do you stop and listen?... What if he's really good? Do you have time for beauty? Shouldn't you?... In a banal setting at an inconvenient time, would beauty transcend?

Weingarten won a Pulitzer proving that it wouldn't: only seven of the thousand-plus that passed paused for a minute or more.

When we go to a concert or stare at a painting that's hanging in a museum, we enter into a relationship: we sign on for the project. We look for beauty, for meaning, for dissonance, for difficulty or artifice. That same piece, encountered elsewhere, can sidle by our conscious minds—but that doesn't mean it escapes our minds completely. It still gets in, past all our walls, and affects us, with or without our
K
N
O
W
I
N
G.

Perhaps in their offices later that morning a few of the people who'd hurried past the busker by the escalator with the scarlet violin paused while making photocopies, or making notes, or making tea, when they felt a whiff of inexplicable pathos.

Said RAUSCHENBERG,

"The
artist's
job
is
to
be
a
witness
to
his
times."

But when artistic techniques escape the museum, artist and times become jumbled; movements and counter-movements, past and present weave themselves to a thing so big it becomes invisible, so intricately sewn its stitches disappear, and which, a huge collage itself, is a different thing at different distances, until the museum is everywhere, until there aren't museums.

Without our best attention, the mess can own us. We own the mess when we consider it, like collages, from various distances, with our most thoughtful scrutiny, the kind we save for art. ✹

Rules for a Composition

P. 47–65

by Brian Roettinger

RULES

1. Use 20%, 50%, 60%, or 70% white space
2. All elements must touch each other
3. Use one image multiple times, at varying scales
4. Use a white background
5. Compose twelve lines, all of different lengths and widths
6. Fill the background with a pattern
7. Fill the background with an image
8. Include a line between one and eight points in thickness
9. Scale image at 200%
10. Scale image at 20%
11. Create a random shape that has no angles. Fill with color or images
12. Create a random shape that has right angles. Fill with color or images
13. Include and arrange between three and twenty images
14. No composed elements can touch each other
15. Compose one image to fill 100% of the page. Remove six random shapes at different sizes from the image
16. Convert an image to halftone
17. Cut the high density area out of an image and discard the area
18. Cut the face out of an image and keep it; discard the rest
19. Cut the face out of an image and discard the face; keep the rest
20. Overlap two images
21. Weight composition towards the top
22. Rotate images five to forty-five degrees
23. Overlap two of the same image
24. Cut the high density area out of an image and fill the area with a new image
25. Cut the high density area out of an image and fill the area with a solid color

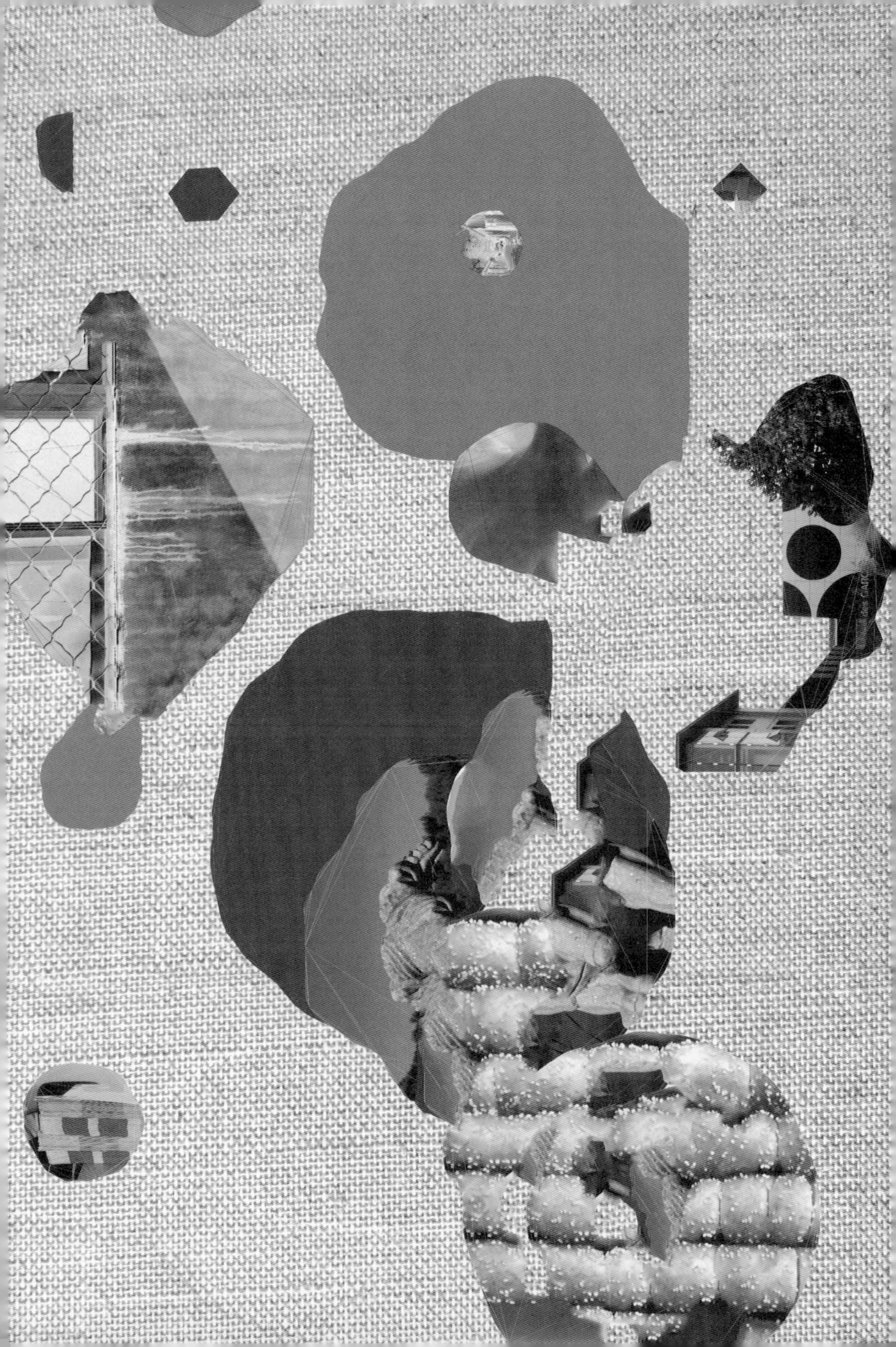

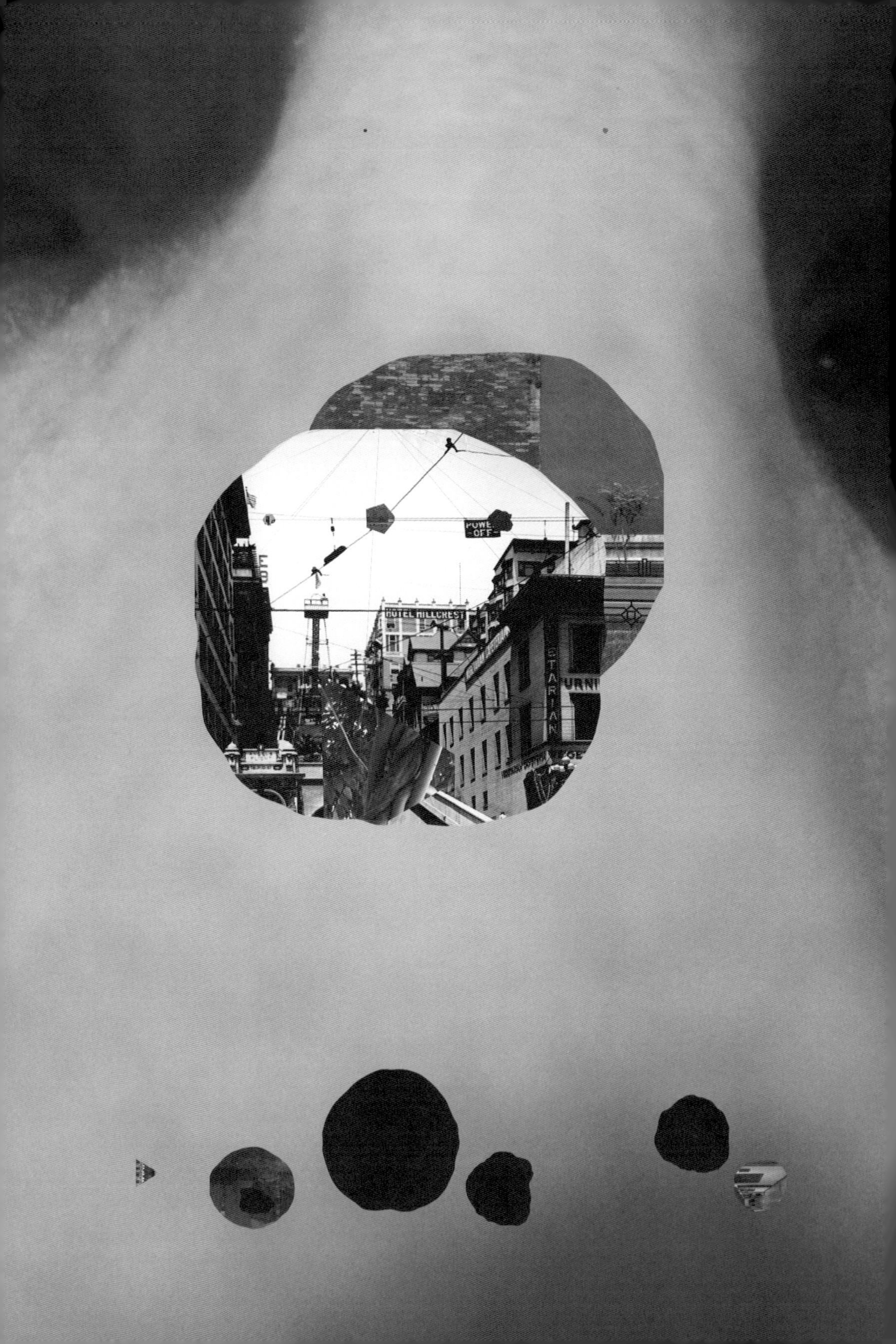
POWE
-OFF-
HOTEL HILLCREST
STARIAN
URNI

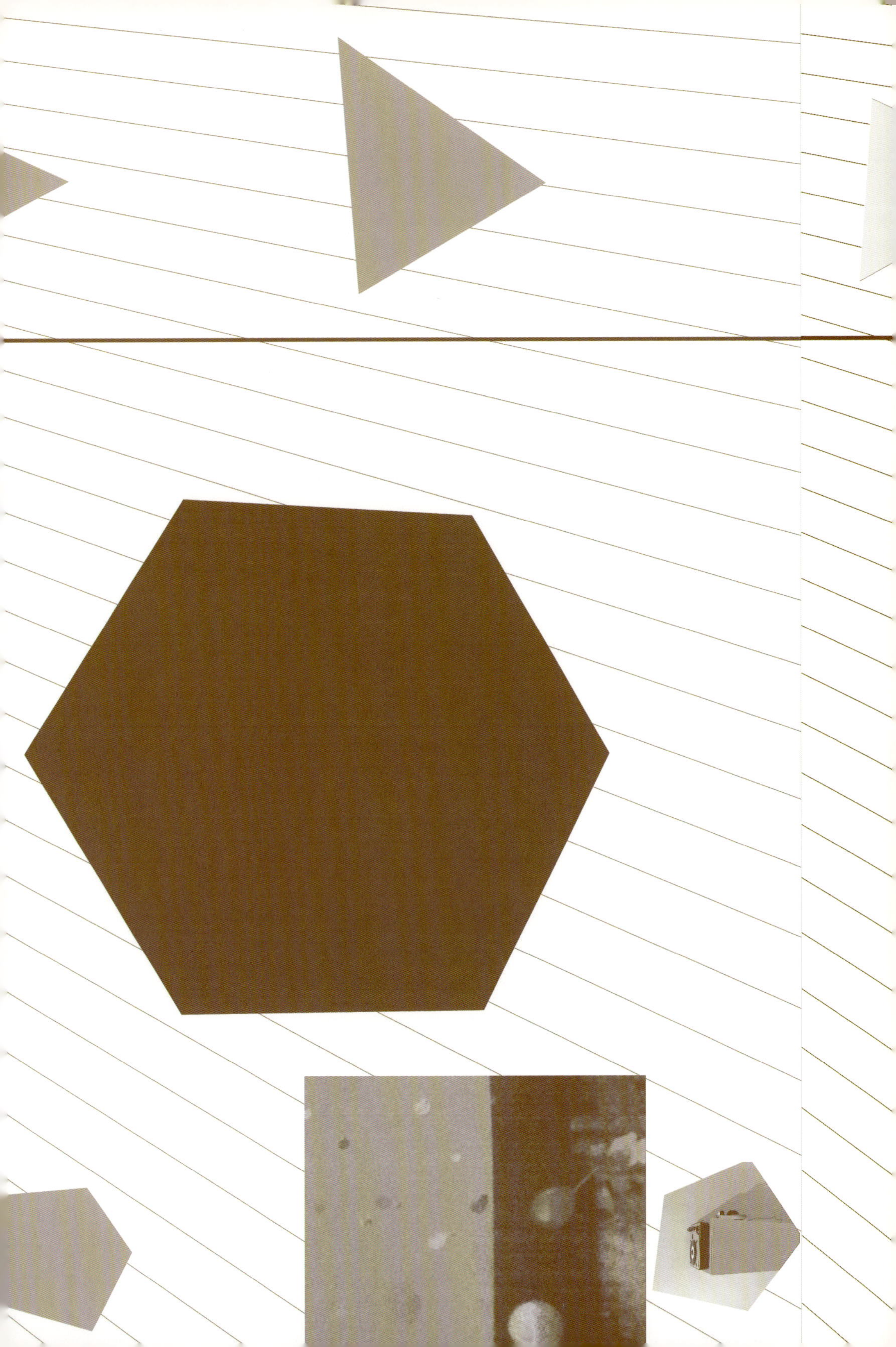

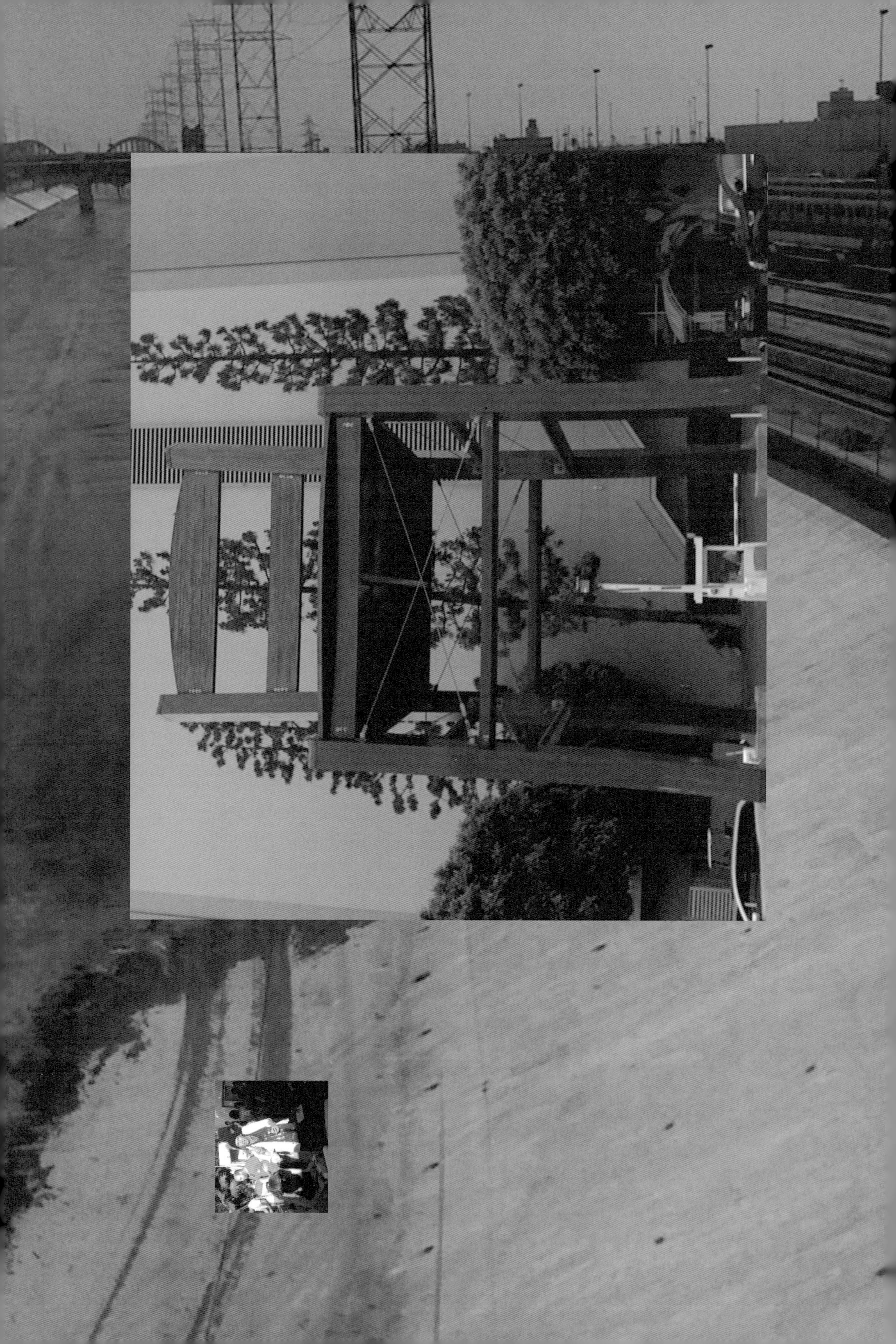

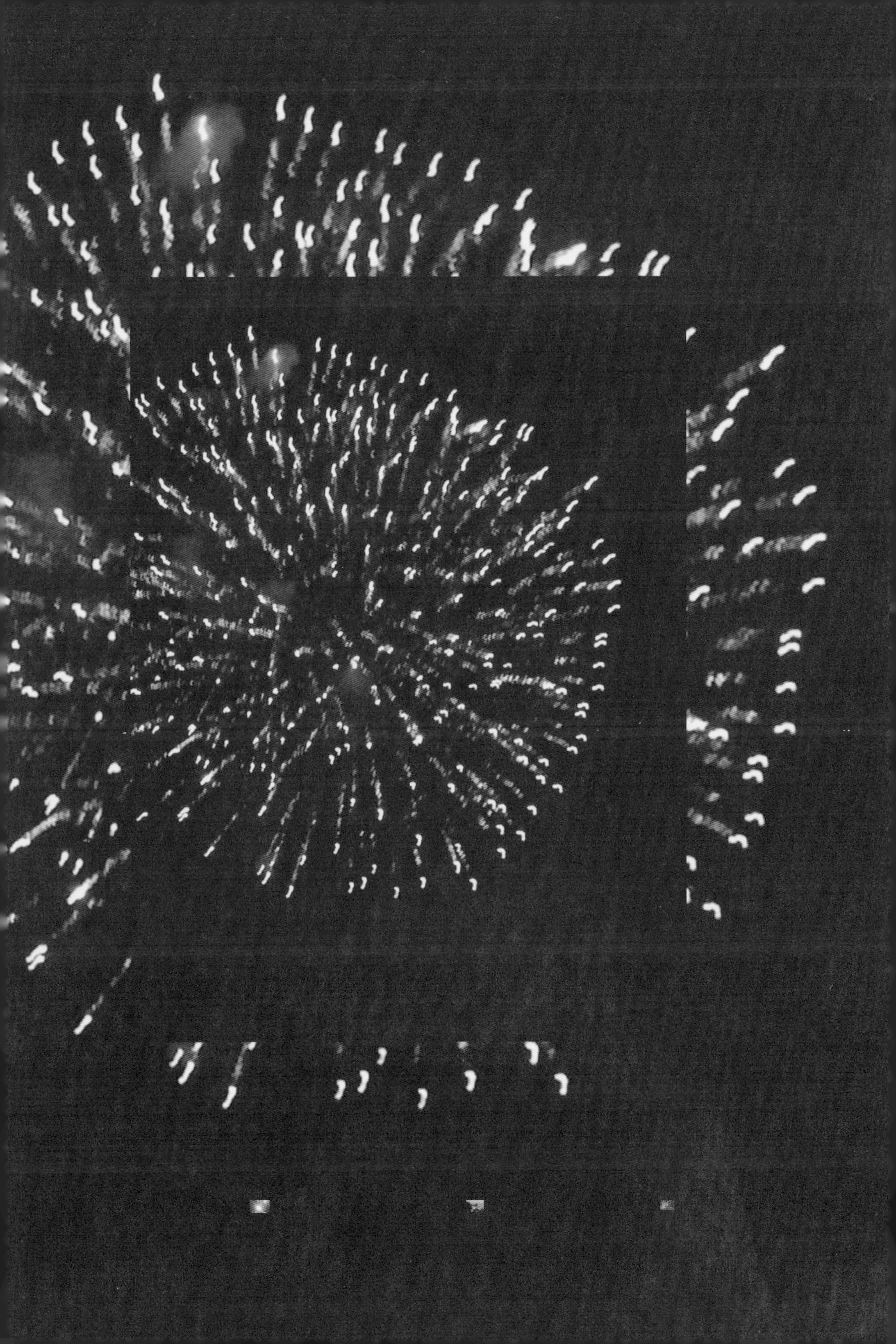

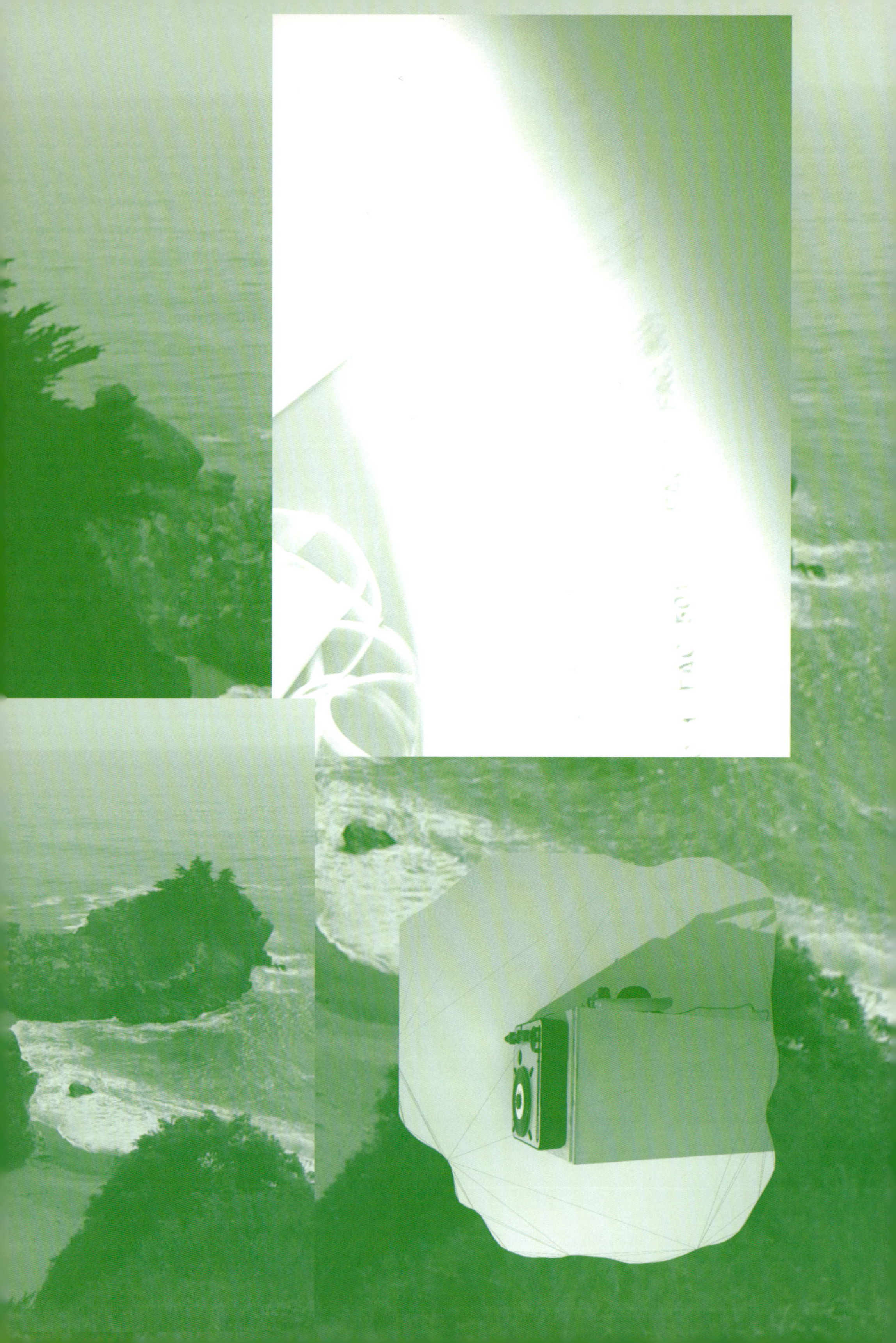

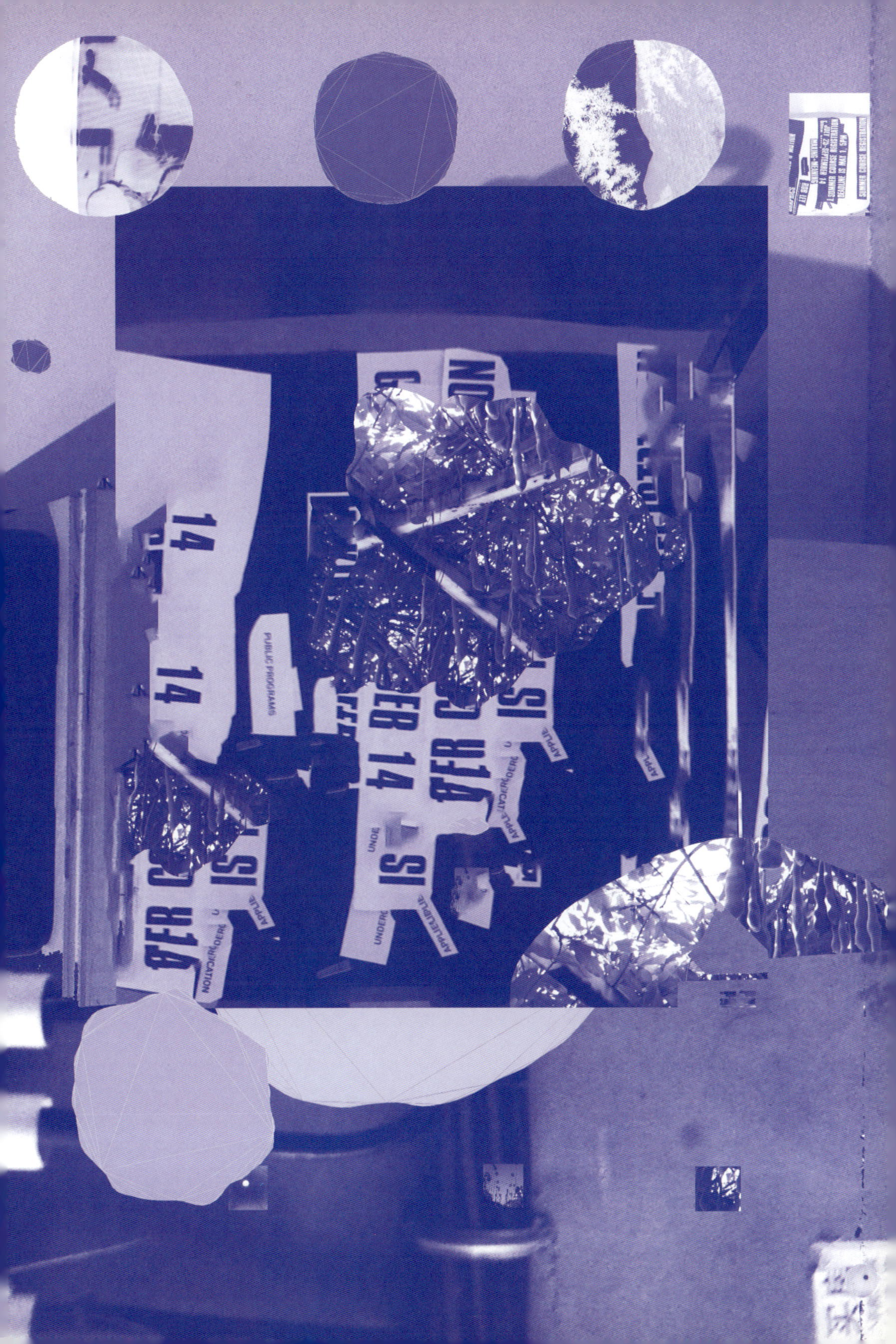

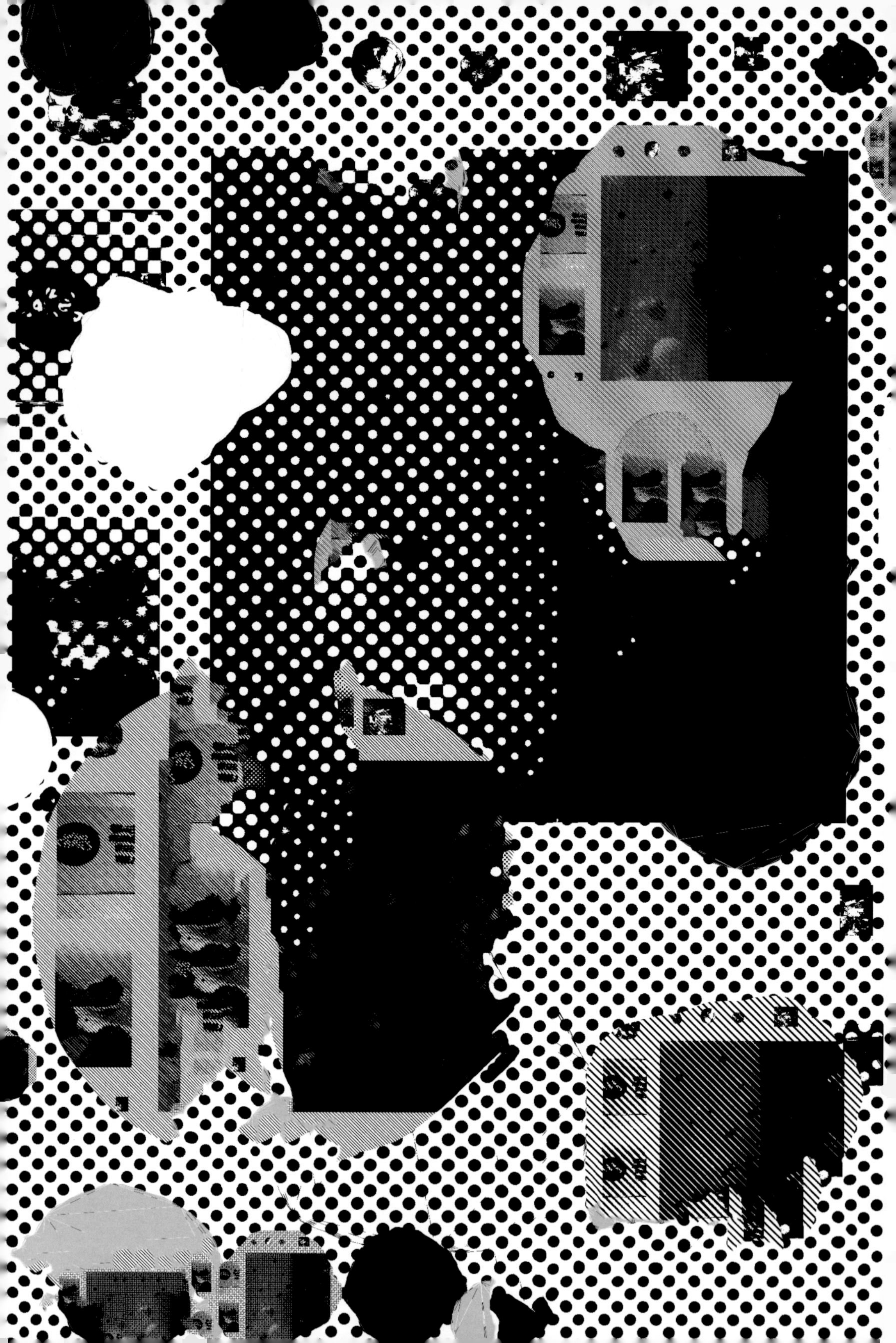

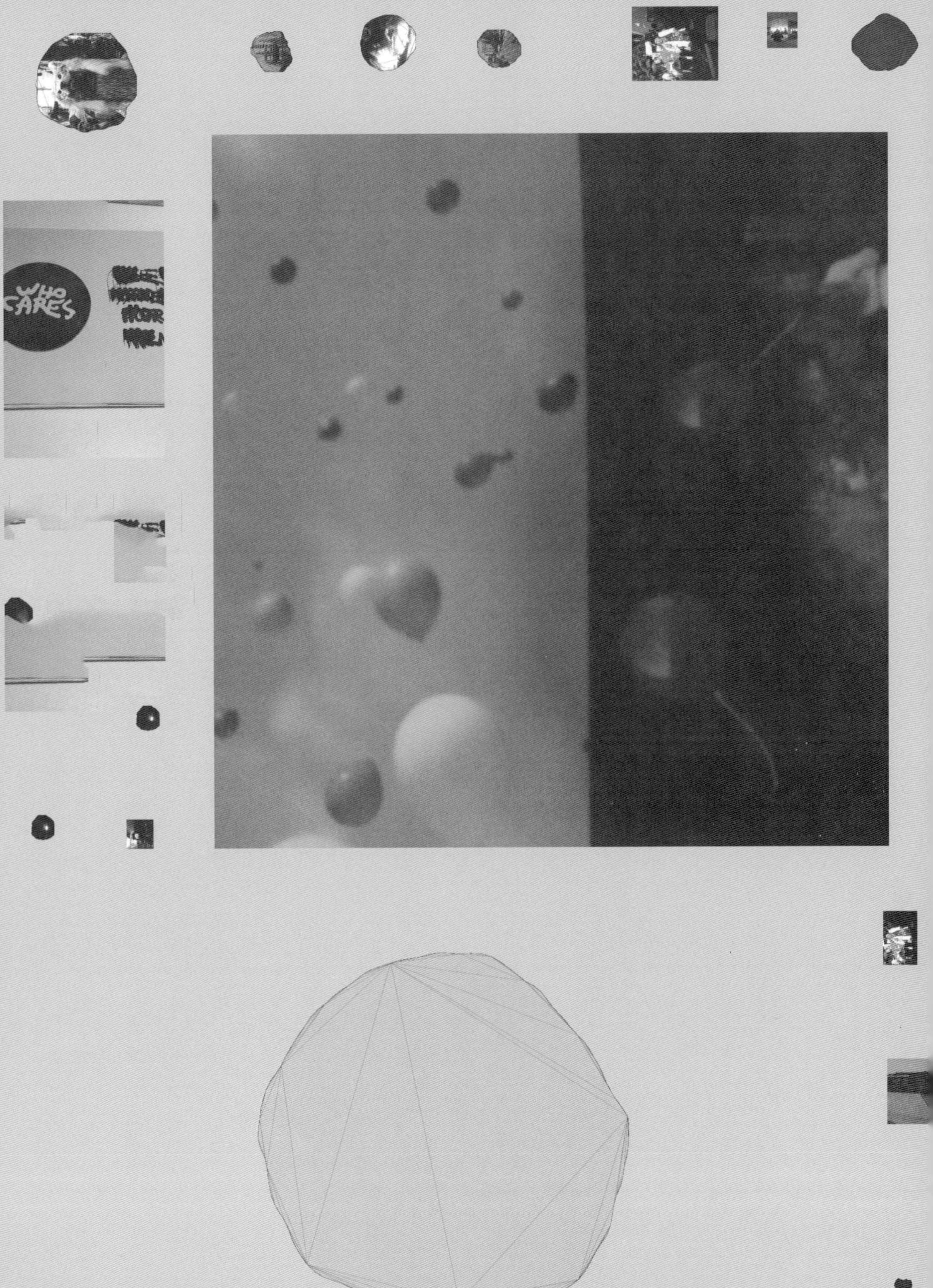
WHO CARES

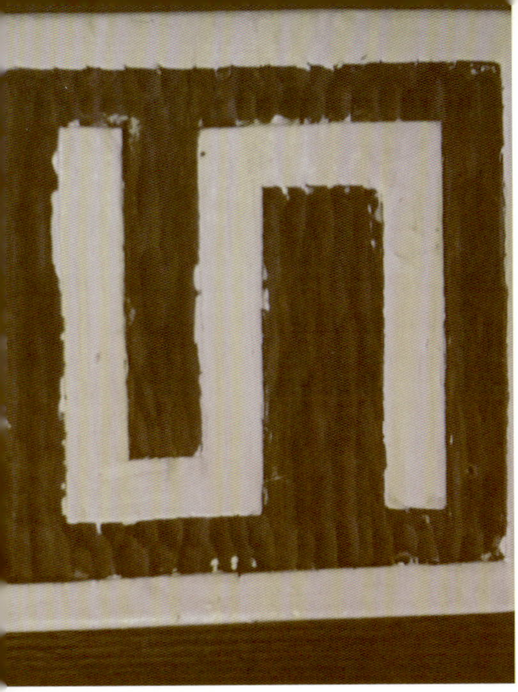
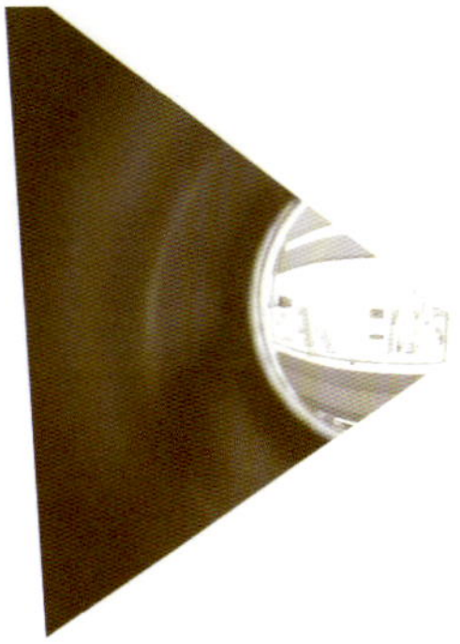
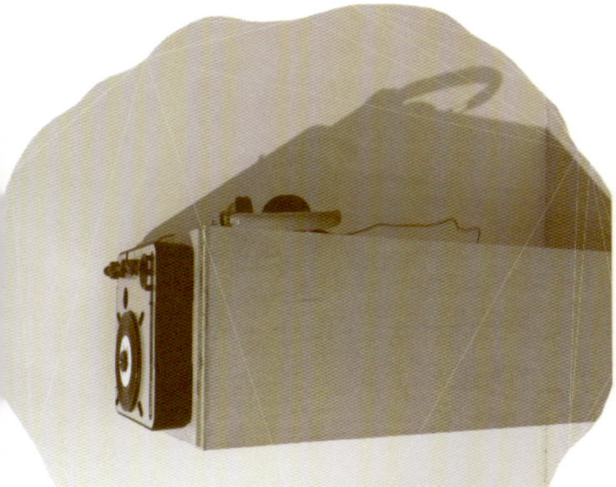
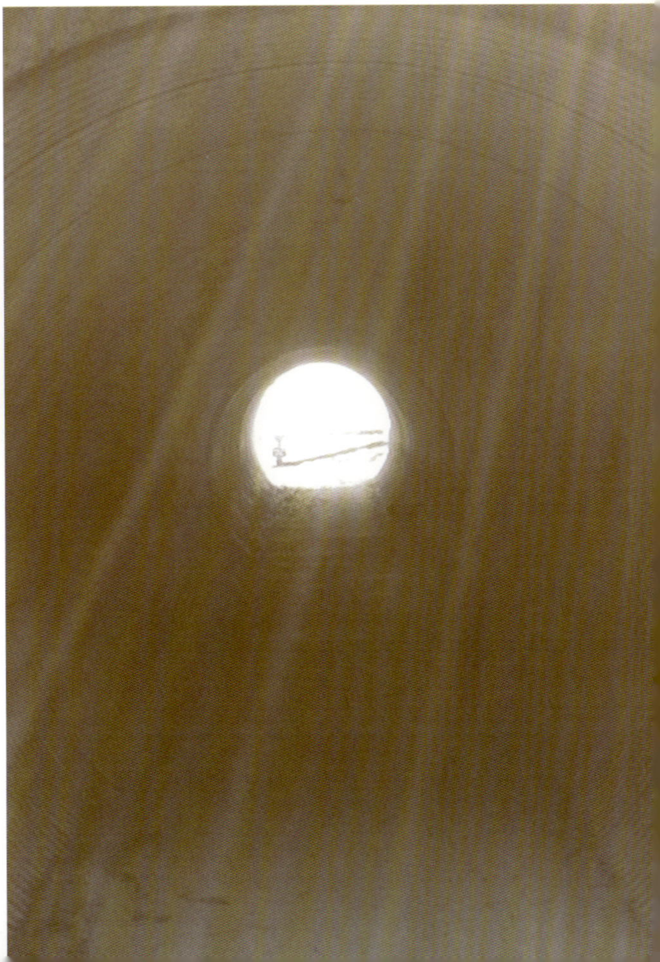

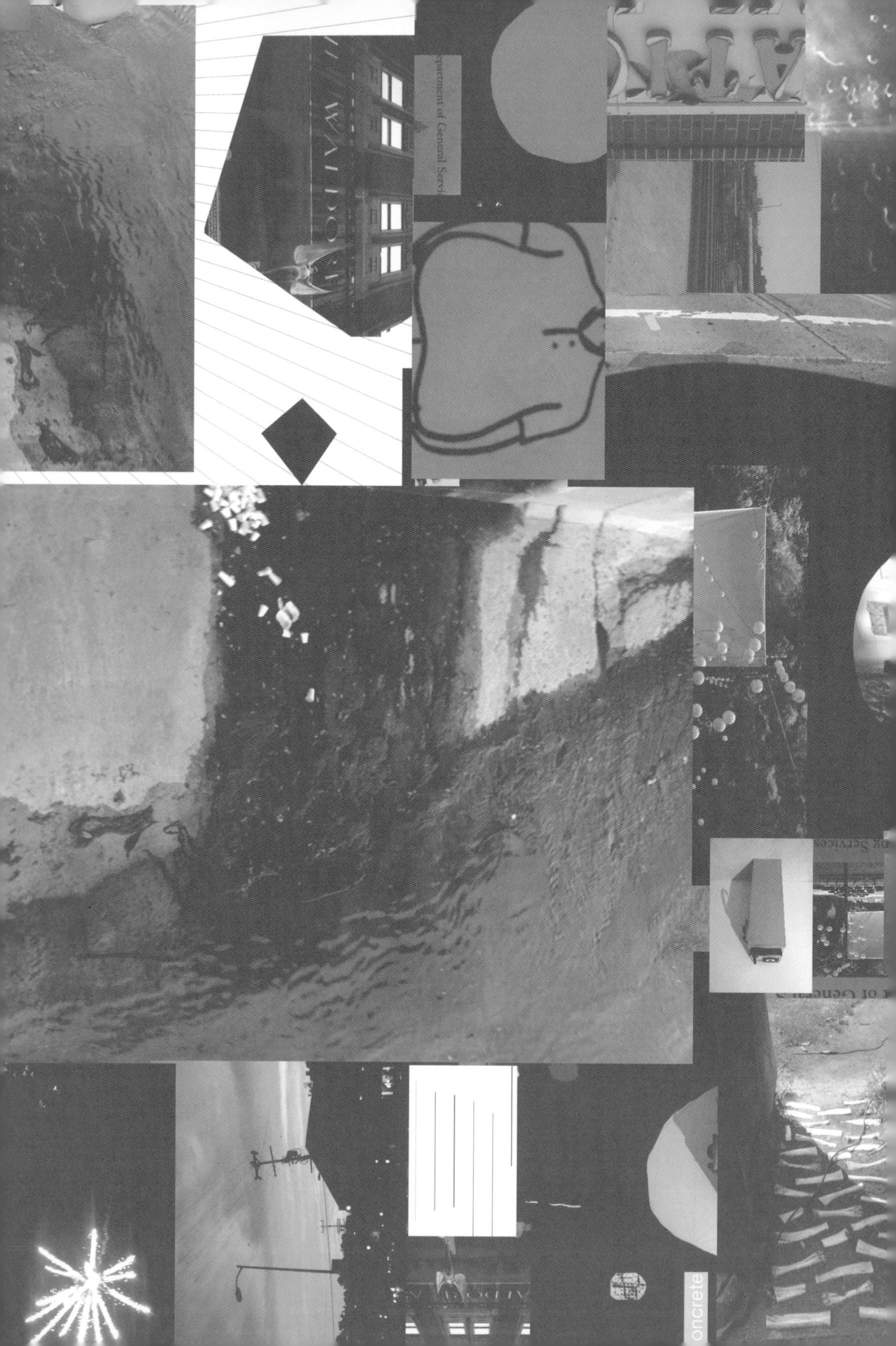
partment of General Servi
oncrete

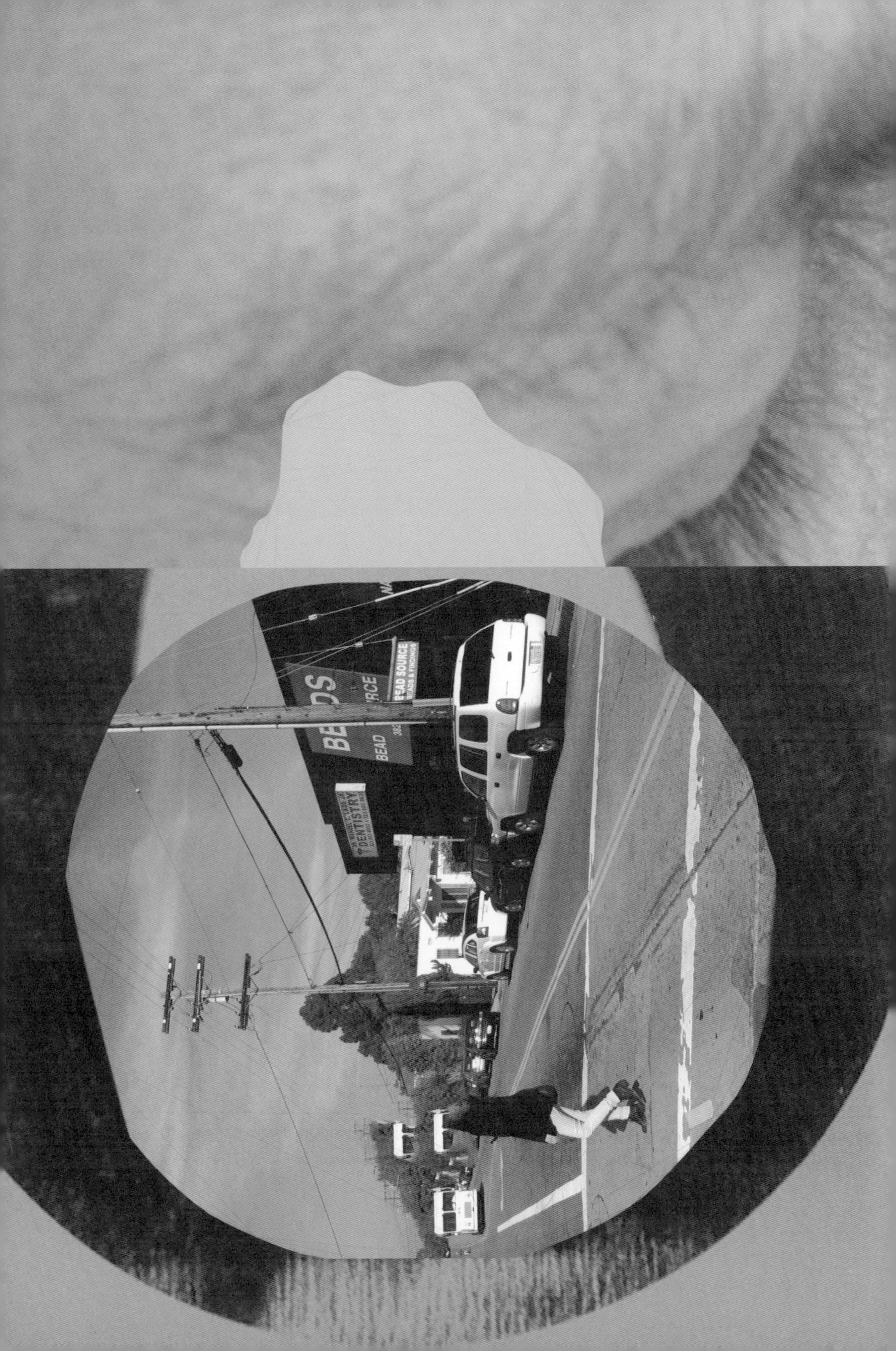
BEAD SOURCE
DENTISTRY

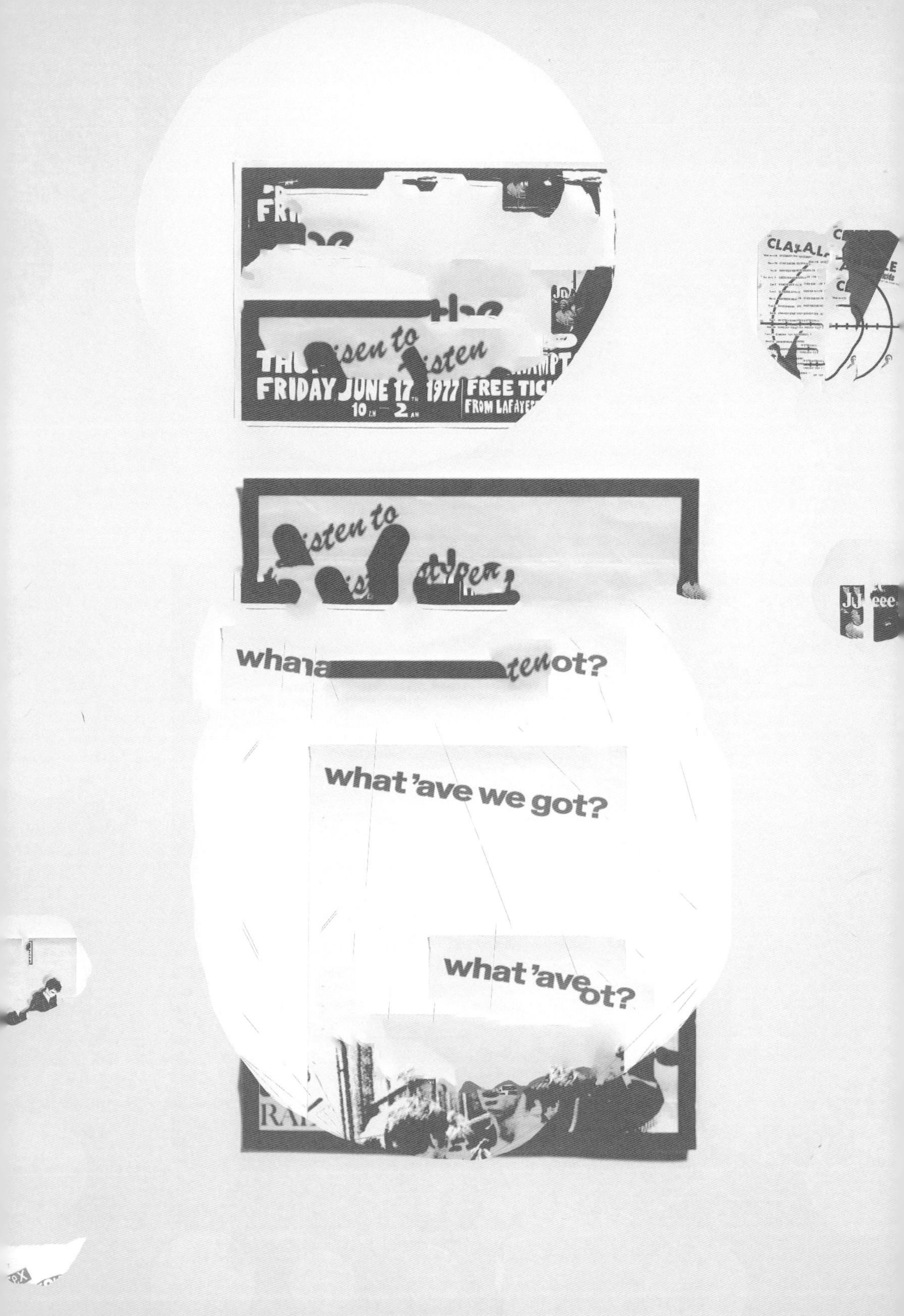
FRIDAY JUNE 17 1977
FREE TIC
what 'ave we got?
what 'ave ot?

1. Rules 1, 9, 10, 11, 13, 17, 18, 20, 22, 25
2. Rules 1, 7, 11, 13
3. Rules 1, 3, 7, 11, 12, 13, 16
4. Rules 1, 2, 7, 11, 19
5. Rules 1, 6, 12, 22
6. Rules 2, 7, 13, 22
7. Rule 23
8. Rules 7, 13, 24
9. Rules 7, 11, 12, 13, 17, 22
10. Rules 6, 11, 13, 16, 22
11. Rules 1, 11, 12, 14, 21
12. Rule 5
13. Rules 1, 4, 12, 13, 14, 22, 24
14. Rules 1, 6, 11, 12, 13
15. Rules 1, 7, 9, 11, 20, 22, 25
16. Rules 1, 7, 10, 23, 24, 25

What will come after the collage era? Pursuing an answer to that question, we asked a handful of artists to create new works entirely devoid of references, as a way of exploring what post-collage might look like. To our initial surprise, more than a few of the artists we approached felt it would be too difficult to make a work that referenced nothing. At which point, we thought: Perhaps what will follow the collage era won't be works without references, it will be works without artists—works that are, essentially, artist-free collages, in which computers do the making. I enlisted the help of programmer/artist Chandler McWilliams; together, he and I developed a list of compositional rules, and he translated these rules into a subsequent collage-making application, which was used to generate the sixteen collages that immediately precede this page.

BRIAN ROETTINGER

The Death of Subculture

P. 67–112

by Aaron Rose

When I was a teenager I happened upon a small independent record store in the San Fernando Valley, the suburban wasteland that lies just outside of metropolitan Los Angeles.

The funky little shop was called Moby Disc.

It was an unassuming storefront
with a cheap, handmade sign,
tucked away in a mini-mall,
across from the shopping center where my mother would drop
my friends and me off to hang out.

WALKING

THROUGH
THE
DOORS

OF THAT PLACE WAS LIKE **OPENING** A PORTAL TO A NEW LIFE.

Before that day I was just a normal kid, DESPERATELY trying to fit in.

But after thumbing through its records and meeting the people who hung out there, I realized that a whole different world existed. IT WAS A WORLD OF NEW IDEAS.

It was a world of fresh and exciting visuals.
It was a world that
I wanted to be
a part of.

One
may
ask
just
what
a
SMALL RECORD SHOP IN THE SUBURBS OF
LOS ANGELES has to do
with the idea that we're living in a "collage culture."

WELL, FOR ME, EVERYTHING.

Moby Disc was an independent record store, which in those days (the mid-1980s) meant it dealt exclusively in SUBCULTURE.

There
were
various
very
defined
subcultures
co-existing
in
SOUTHERN CALIFORNIA at that time, and small record stores like Moby Disc served as adjunct clubhouses for them.

It was there that I first learned about teenage cultural movements such as

PUNK

NEW WAVE

GOTH

NEW ROMANTIC

MOD

SKA

SKINHEAD

ROCKABILLY

and a host of other small cultural sub-sects that were very distinctly defined not only by music and style, but, most importantly, by a shared way of interpreting the world.

Viewpoints were very
distinct
from
group
to
group

but there was a collective ethos through the whole community that was ROOTED IN BEING AN OUTSIDER.

No matter how small any particular group was, subcultures were a way for kids like me to define ourselves. They served as catalysts for identity-building and helped us to understand where we stood in relation to the status quo.

Now, over ten years into the first decade of a new millennium, it's quite tempting for me to lament the loss of the innocence of those days, but my appreciation for that time is more than just nostalgia. It can't be denied that the era of clearly defined and distinct youth subcultures is behind us.

N
O
W, instead, we have a CREATIVE CULTURE BASED ON A HYBRIDIZATION OF STYLES.

The 21st-century Western world has become a blender devouring the trends of the last century, and in it, all styles have become one. As a result of this process, a sense of originality has been L O S T , and the current generation of youth has had to pay the price.

We are in danger of destroying the fundamental and basic foundations of our creative identity. Our culture has come to view the tenets of original thought and creative innovation as an outdated model—but it has yet to release a new version that replaces it. At one point in time, wearing a certain style of clothing or listening to a certain genre of music came with a personal mission statement. When all these styles mix together, as they do today, the original ideologies are lost in the shuffle. Personal politics are absent and what we are left with is an utter sense of confusion. So what has caused this confusion? The answer, partly, lies in our current overwhelming access to digital information. Meaning that, at this particular time in the collective consciousness, the availability of past images and references is unprecedented. However, this isn't the entire answer—there's more to it than that.

> The past went that-a-way. When faced with a totally new situation, we tend always to attach ourselves to the objects, to the flavor of the most recent past. We look at the present through a rear view mirror. We march backwards into the future.
>
> **– Marshall McLuhan** [1]

To say our society's current information overdose is the only root cause of this problem is just too easy.

Yes, at the click of a mouse we can instantly find photographic reference material for any era since the invention of the camera. The muddling effect of this wealth of information is undeniable and it's logical to suggest that this could become culturally confusing.

However, alongside those images are almost always

pages
and
pages
and
pages
and
pages
and
pages
and

and
pages
and
pages
and
pages
and
pages
and
pages

pages
and
pages
and
pages
and
pages
and
pages
and

of texts, documents and personal anecdotes from original sources that support and explain the ideologies of each and every one of these subcultural developments. So the question here is, Why, in an era when we have access to all this history, both

visual and

philosophical,

do we choose as a society to take only the VISUAL REFERENCES and to abandon the IDEOLOGICAL ONES?

When I visited Moby Disc in the 80s, it felt like I was doing something dangerous. The ideas embedded in each and every one of those records, books and even t-shirts had the power to rip open everything I believed in.

THE VISUALS WERE THE FIRST THING THAT HOOKED ME

but once I sat down and played the record I would pore over the liner notes, study the back of the album jacket and try to glean any kind of knowledge possible.

The information I was being exposed to was deeply controversial and generally flew in the face of all I'd been taught. I knew I was abandoning all notions of ever being the same again.

[I WAS HAVING A GENUINE EXPERIENCE.]

On the racks of that shop I had found a world where being different was normal, a place where the outcast was the hero.

The loser became beautiful.

Being "anti" didn't necessarily mean being nihilistic, at least not in any serious way, but it did suggest that the world that I had been sold by the government, my parents and schools was no longer relevant to a lifestyle that I wanted to lead. I had received a cultural get-out-of-jail-free card and I accepted it with an immense gratitude the likes of which I had never come close to before in my life.

From that day on I was truly SUBCULTURAL.

> The word "subculture" is loaded down with mystery. It suggests secrecy, masonic oaths, an Underworld. It also invokes the larger and no less difficult concept "culture." So it is with the idea of culture that we should begin.
>
> **– Dick Hebdige** [2]

★ ★ ★ ★ ★ ★ ★

THE GREATEST IDEAS IN HISTORY HAVE ALWAYS BEEN AT FIRST DISMISSED AS THE RANTINGS OF MADMEN. IF SOMEONE IS OSTRACIZED, UNPOPULAR, EVEN JAILED FOR THEIR BELIEFS, THEY ARE SOMEONE TO WHOM WE SHOULD PAY CLOSE ATTENTION.

★ ★ ★ ★ ★ ★ ★

While some might construe our penchant for excluding our best thinkers as

a negative, it is

exactly the **opposite**.

The outcasts in our world know something very important. In fact, it is just this exclusion that actually fuels their fires of dissent.

FROM REBELLION
OFTEN COMES
NEW IDEAS.

As a result of this CULTURAL SEGREGATION, society actually breeds lifestyles that can develop entirely free from common cultural influence.

Within this netherworld of societal disdain, a schattenreich of immense intellectual freedom develops. Therefore I propose that some kind of forced exile, be it real or metaphorical, from the popular cultural and media dialogue is key and absolutely necessary for the progression

of

human

creative

growth.

The 20th century's most significant subcultural developments matured in isolation. If you look at the current Jazz culture, the common perception is that it has been completely stripped of its countercultural roots. However, at its birth in the late 1940s, the musical form was the definition of derelict. It was centered around a small strip of nightclubs on 5th Avenue and 52nd Street in New York City, a neighborhood that "provided shelter for fringe denizens of Broadway-sign-painters and private detectives." [3]

A decade later, the Beat Generation developed around City Lights Books, a forgettable little shop in San Francisco, eventually setting the stage for what would become Haight-Ashbury, another small community—one which became the countercultural center of the 1960s.

Although fraught with its own set of problems, the ethos of the Haight Street community seemed to be freedom and organic individuality. They felt one could only be free by "drawing the line and living outside the profit, private property, and power premises of Western culture." [4]

AS JAZZ WAS DEVELOPING, A GROUP OF ARTISTS DRANK TOGETHER
AT A RUNDOWN OLD WATERING HOLE CALLED
THE CEDAR TAVERN IN NEW YORK CITY.

This group, which went on to be called the

A	T	E	I
B		X	O
S		P	N
T		R	I
R		E	S
A		S	T
C		S	S,

quietly developed a major underground notoriety without drawing any notice from the surrounding mainstream culture. Today, ABSTRACT EXPRESSIONISM is noted as one of the most important artistic movements of the 20th century, but back then it was just a small group of people expressing new ideas. The Cedar Tavern was a dank, musty room where the dark side gathered and a place that respectable people were encouraged to avoid.

This story of cultural dissent—and subcultures developing in shadowy corners—continued throughout the 20th century ad infinitum. In the 1970s it was the

PUNKS.

The PUNK X SUBCULTURE associated with Southern California was an anomaly unlike anything I had ever seen.

THE FIRST TIME I SAW A KID WITH A MOHAWK WALKING DOWN THE STREETS OF MY SUBURBAN NEIGHBORHOOD MY REACTION WAS A COMBINATION OF TOTAL INSPIRATION AND ABSOLUTE FEAR.

The sheer courage that it took to dress and act that way, in a fashion so completely adversarial to one's environment, was mind-blowing to me. The punks in California were complete aliens, strange and magical creatures that found hangouts in neon-lit convenience store parking lots and lonely tract community cul-de-sacs. These misfit kids and the culture that surrounded them became my Rosetta Stone.

There used to be an underground bookstore in Los Angeles called Amok. I can't exactly remember how I found this place. It was on the corner of Sunset and Hyperion in Los Angeles, which now hosts a collection of trendy eateries and hip shops, but back then it was a pretty rough neighborhood. If I remember correctly the store had no sign. Inside there were books about bomb-making, counterintelligence, civil disobedience, drugs, sex, devil-worship and just about every conspiracy theory known to man. It became my own City Lights, another hub where my personal understanding of subculture was born.

Every time I went to Amok
I
would
come
home
with
a
stack
of
books,
which I would then devour in my bedroom when I was supposed to be asleep. The information I was receiving became as important to me as the countercultural fashions that defined my look. The style and substance were inseparable. One could credit this store with educating an entire generation of young Southern Californian outsiders.

So how did almost all of the most significant cultural movements of the last hundred years end up developing in such squalid locations?

EACH AND EVERY SUBCULTURE HAS DEVELOPED IN A PLACE FREE FROM THE PRYING EYES OF THE GENERAL POPULACE.

~~~~~~~~~~~~~~ THERE WAS MOST CERTAINLY ALWAYS AN AUDIENCE,

but it was comprised of a
small group
of like-minded peers
who were perpetrating the same crimes.

In today's climate, however, small communities that spawn influential subcultures would be impossibly difficult to cultivate. The world is simply too connected. It is virtually impossible to remain obscure in today's constant information exchange. The incubator is broken, the audience is too big, and even if the baby is premature, it is quickly paraded in front of the cameras.

But perhaps it's not that the audience has grown that's the problem—maybe it's that the audience is missing.
~~~~~~~~~~~~~~

As consumers of cyber culture, we are continually dealing with what I would describe as an

"INVISIBLE AUDIENCE."

Meaning that while there may be thousands and thousands of people contributing to and viewing our collective history through their computers, nobody is actually present in that encounter.

YOU CAN GOOGLE YOUR WAY TO INFORMATION, BUT YOU CANNOT GOOGLE AN EXPERIENCE.

AT LEAST NOT YET.

And perhaps this is where the real death of subculture takes place.

> If we are to achieve a richer culture, rich in contrasting values, we must recognize the whole gamut of human potentialities, and so weave a less arbitrary social fabric, one in which each diverse gift will find a fitting place.
>
> **– Margaret Mead** [5]

So how can we, as 21st-century humans, maneuver this changing landscape and continue to remain CULTURALLY PROGRESSIVE? Perhaps by asking this question we can find clues to why we live in this collage culture, and in the process possibly find new, uncharted avenues that could lead mankind to a greater sense of identity, both individually and as a group. Jumping off the information superhighway isn't enough. A culture would have to be truly underground, releasing itself not only from the world of documentation, but the world of the media culture as a whole. One way of doing this would be to somehow create the effect of isolation without having to actually detach. Cutting ourselves off from media culture would not only be a mistake, but also nearly impossible.

We must find a way to create a metaphorical incubator within this landscape in which true individual identities can spawn.

One might imagine that using the avenues of social networking to create an online community of outsiders would solve this problem, but it wouldn't—an online community does not provide the direct person-to-person experience needed to properly manifest new culture.

We somehow need to

The ugly words. The forbidden words, the accursed words, the words covered with blood, the dangerous words, the words that do not belong to the dictionary…

– Jean Genet [6]

WHERE ARE THE "UGLY" WORDS NOW?

THEY MUST EXIST.

Even the most jaded old soul can't be nearly so bleak as to assume that nobody has an original thought anymore. Perhaps the only way a new and wholly unique subculture could ever develop in the 21st century is by placing itself completely outside the confines of the documentable world. However, there are very few places that still allow this freedom. Taking a cue from Genet, the prison system comes to mind. Until recently, our penal institutions were perhaps amongst the last bastions of true media isolation left in the Western world (though now many prisoners can get online and some even have blogs).

But—while somewhat romantic—proposing that the only true cultural progressions possible in the 21st century would have to come from a world without access is not a logical solution.

I'm not necessarily proposing that one needs scribble out manifestos on toilet paper from a jail cell to be countercultural. But perhaps we should look at the ideas central to living as an outlaw and try to be less literal.

Learn to say "Fuck You" to the world once in a while. You have every right to. Just stop thinking, worrying, looking over your shoulder wondering, doubting, fearing, hurting, hoping for some easy way out, struggling, grasping, confusing, itchin, scratching, mumbling, bumbling, grumbling, humbling, stumbling, numbling, rumbling, gambling, tumbling, scumbling, scrambling, hitching, hatching, bitching, moaning, groaning, honing, boning, horse-shitting, hair-splitting, nit-picking, piss-trickling, nose sticking, ass-gouging, eyeball-poking, finger-pointing, alleyway-sneaking, long waiting, small stepping, evil-eyeing, back-scratching, searching, perching, besmirching, grinding, grinding, grinding away at yourself. Stop it and just DO!... Don't worry about cool, make your own uncool. Make your own, your own world.

– Sol LeWitt to Eva Hesse, 1965 [7]

The word "laws" most often brings to mind a set of penal codes established by society and government for the good of a balanced civilization. But what if we were to look at this concept from an internal perspective? What if we as creative beings started to restructure inwardly in the sense that by breaking our own internal laws, which were established by fear and insecurity and a need to conform, we may open ourselves up to just the breakthrough we are looking for? We need not harm anyone in this quest, nor can we be jailed for it. We become our own cultural outlaws who are in turn rewriting the rules.

As a result we simply free ourselves from the desire to hunt, borrow and use that has created this collage in favor of a healthy and passionate yen to invent what's next.

Some members of my
generation seem to have
an insatiable hunger for
the most hard-to-find
specimens of creative
culture from the
previous century.

I cannot tell you how
many times I've listened
to people eagerly exclaim
about some rare record
or some forgotten artist
as though it were the latest
development in culture.

I'm not suggesting that searching for rare gems is always a bad thing. However, a generation seeking identity through an obsession with obscurities from the past is missing the point.

There's a general belief within the HIPSTER SET that somehow in that rarity something new can be found—but what's actually happening is nothing but a facsimile of revolt. Even though the proposed references are uncommon, the collage still perpetuates and culture again eats itself. We can, however, find an organic way to manufacture our own obscurity. There is no greater feeling in life than stumbling upon something original. However, this sensation need not always be motivated by something from the past. Each and every one of us has the power within ourselves to find a truly original path.

All ———— this ———— requires———— is a bit ———— of courage ———— and a ———— willingness ———— to forget ———— what we know.

WHEN ONE ADOPTS A PHILOSOPHY OF INNOVATION, CREATING NEW THINGS BECOMES ALMOST SECOND NATURE. It is something that is not thought of or talked about. It is just done. The only hope for true cultural freedom is to stop imitating the trends of the 20th century; from there, the rest will work itself out. Of course, when one begins this kind of quest some initial floundering is inevitable and errors will certainly be made. But those so-called mistakes are only a negative thing when they are assessed according to the paradigms of the past. If we are able to throw away those old, outdated modes of judgment then maybe those wrongs could actually become rights. As James Joyce famously said, "A man's errors are his portals of discovery." If we put aside our fear and consciously decide that we refuse to copy and continue to push through this, we may actually create a new culture. Once we become free from the imitation of the past, new areas of exploration will open up to us and suddenly this new millennium will finally develop a distinct identity all its own.

> Technology is destructive only in the hands of people who do not realize that they are one and the same process as the universe.
>
> **– Alan Watts** [8]

There is one present-day community that could serve as a good model of invention for the wider culture at large.

Computer programmers and those in the technology sector are not interested in finding the rarest 1950s toaster and then making cheap reproductions of it. With few exceptions, the primary focus for all computer scientists is creating new and exciting ways for human beings to have easier, better lives. Think about the possibilities if as a culture we were able to apply this approach to our cultural or subcultural lives.

What if, before every cultural action we took, we were to ask ourselves, "How could this make my world better?"

BY ACTUALLY
MAKING DECISIONS
BASED ON WHAT COULD
ENRICH OUR OWN PERSONAL
SPHERES, WE ARE BY DEFAULT
CREATING A MORE INTERESTING
EXPERIENCE FOR EVERYONE
AROUND US.

Everything in the world is somehow based on things that have come before and technology is no different.

However, instead of recycling old technologies, repackaging and selling them back to us as modern, the technology sector thrives because a culture has been created around it that applauds the most innovative minds.

Many times these breakthroughs are controversial. Sometimes they are even extreme failures, yet still they are allowed to exist because even though a certain idea may not be perfect, there is a general feeling within that community that there is still a chance there for further discovery. Imagine if we could look at all the mistakes we make as a creative culture in the same way.

I feel quite excited for the future of our civilization and I believe that our greatest breakthroughs in art, music, film, and literature are certainly yet to come.

To bring this about, the age of the collage should finally come to a close. New shapes are fighting to be born and we must loosen the hard and cracked surface that refuses to let them sprout. SUBCULTURE AS WE KNEW IT MAY BE DEAD. But as Glen O'Brien recently said to me as we waited for a bathroom together one evening in Marfa, Texas, "SUBCULTURE IS NO SUBSTITUTE FOR CULTURE."

Subculture exists to incubate, but when we live in a world where slow gestation is no longer an option we are forced to manage our expectations.

We must instead strive to lead a total existence of innovation.

In the 20th century small subcultures existed to serve a purpose that was specific to that era. The needs of this new millennium are different, and we must find a new way forward that reflects this fact.

Without leaps of imagination, or dreaming, we lose the excitement of possibilities. Dreaming, after all, is a form of planning.

– Gloria Steinem [9]

As we plan for this new reality, we need not murder the past—

BUT THE PAST MUST NO LONGER SERVE AS OUR MASTER.

The time is here to take control of this new millennium and to embrace all its gifts. References to eras past are the building blocks with which we can create something new—not as a copy, but as a truly original manifestation of the multilayered existence we all now share. There is no reason why each and every one of us cannot be continually having experiences like the one I had as a thirteen-year-old at Moby Disc. We deserve to live lives full of inspiration and wonder at every turn. The resources are there for us, and with only a small shift in our perception, the way forward is **right before our eyes.** ✸

FOOTNOTES

1.
Marshall McLuhan, The Medium is the Massage, London: Penguin Books, 1967. At the time of its publishing, The Medium is the Massage sparked a subcultural movement of its own. It's interesting to consider that McLuhan was already addressing some of the issues we raise here at a time when information was much harder to access than it is today.

2.
Dick Hebdige, Subculture: The Meaning of Style, Methuen & Co. Ltd, 1979. In this seminal work, Hebdige argues that progressive thought must always be at first unpopular, even criminal.

3.
Lewis MacAdams, Birth of the Cool: Beat, Bebop and the American Avant-Garde, New York: The Free Press, 2001. The entire selection here reads: "The upper stories, which earlier in the century had housed upwardly-mobile, middle-class families, now provided shelter for fringe denizens of Broadway-sign-painters and private detectives and the freelance 'shooters' who, their pockets stuffed with flashbulbs, prowled the neighborhood nightclubs looking for a picture that they could sell... The ground floors and damp basements had been converted into tiny nightspots—the Downbeat, the Spotlite, Kelly's Stables, the Yacht Club, the Famous Door, and a half-dozen more—some no bigger than apartment living rooms, charging stiff prices for watered-down cocktails. On any night, you could hear virtually the entire history of jazz from New Orleans and Dixieland to swing and bebop as you walked up and down the street—'The Street.'" Tenor Dexter Gordon called that street "unquestionably, the most exciting half-block in the world" in Ira Gitler's Jazz Masters of the 40s. Said Gordon: "Everything was going on—music, chicks, connections—so many musicians working down there side by side."

4.
Emmett Grogan, Ringolevio: A Life Played for Keeps, Little, Brown, 1972. An interesting side note here is that even at the height of the 1960s counterrevolution, Grogan, the founder of the Diggers, still had his doubts about the ability of subculture to really change anything. The entire selection reads: "These discussions that Billy, Emmett, and the others had, dealt with the freedom being assumed by young people in Haight-Ashbury and throughout the world. They agreed that the ultimate goal of the Haight community seemed to be freedom and a chance to do your thing, but they felt one could only be free by drawing the line and living outside the profit, private property, and power premises of Western culture because, as Coyote remarked, 'The idea of changing anything from within has been exploded long ago.'"

5.
Margaret Mead, excerpt taken from Sex and Temperament: In Three Primitive Societies (1935). This text became a major cornerstone of the feminist movement since it claims that females are dominant in the Tchambuli Lake region of Papua New Guinea without it causing any special problems.

6.
Jean Genet, from the introduction to Soledad Brother: The Prison Letters of George Jackson, New York: Coward-McCann, 1970. George Jackson was convicted of armed robbery at age eighteen, and was sentenced to serve one year to life in prison. While at San Quentin in 1966, he founded the Black Guerilla Family, a Marxist prison gang with political objectives. On January 16, 1970, he was charged with murdering a prison guard. Incarcerated in the maximum security cellblock at Soledad Prison, Jackson and the other two inmates became known as the Soledad Brothers. In solitary confinement for twenty-three hours a day, Jackson studied political economy and radical theory. On August 21, 1971, three days before he was to go on trial, twenty-nine-year-old George Jackson was shot and killed at San Quentin prison in what was alleged by prison officials to be an escape attempt. French intellectuals including Michel Foucault and Jean Genet argued that Jackson's death was a political assassination.

7.
Sol LeWitt, from a letter he wrote to Eva Hesse dated April 14, 1965. The meeting of Eva Hesse and Sol LeWitt in 1960 sparked a decade-long friendship that led to a fervent dialogue. For both, art meant everything, but with Hesse, self-doubt was a constant companion. In 1965, to encourage her when she found herself particularly challenged during the year she spent in Germany, LeWitt wrote this letter. Whether LeWitt's words elevated Hesse's spirits is something we can't know, but as an emotional declaration of conviction, they remain timeless and inspirational for anyone devoted to the creative process.

8.
Alan Watts, from The Book: On the Taboo Against Knowing Who You Are, Vintage, San Francisco, 1966. For more than forty years, Alan Watts earned a reputation as a leading interpreter of Eastern philosophies for the West. Beginning at age sixteen, he developed an audience of millions who were enriched through his books, tape recordings, public lectures and television and radio work. Watts wrote more than twenty-five books and recorded hundreds of lectures and seminars—an astonishing output that can be matched in volume by few philosophers.

9.
Quote by Gloria Steinem. Original source unknown (even to Steinem herself). Gloria Steinem is an American journalist and social and political activist who became nationally recognized as a leader of, and media spokeswoman for, the women's liberation movement in the late 1960s and 1970s. In 1972, she co-founded Ms. magazine, and remained one of its editors for fifteen years. She was instrumental in the magazine's move to join and be published by the Feminist Majority Foundation. In 1968, she helped to found New York magazine, where she soon became an incendiary political columnist.

Texts
Aaron Rose & Mandy Kahn

Design
Brian Roettinger

Typeface
SuperGrotesk, Times BQ, Letter Gothic

Proofreading
Clare Manchester

Color Separation & Print
Musumeci S.p.A., Quart (Aosta)

Printed in Europe

Published by

JRP|Ringier
Letzigraben 134
CH-8047 Zurich
T +41 (0) 43 311 27 50
F +41 (0) 43 311 27 51
E info@jrp-ringier.com
www.jrp-ringier.com

JRP|Ringier books are available internationally at selected bookstores and from the following distribution partners:

Switzerland
AVA Verlagsauslieferung AG, Centralweg 16, CH-8910 Affoltern a.A.
verlagsservice@ava.ch
www.ava.ch

France
Les presses du réel, 35 rue Colson, F-21000 Dijon info@lespressesdureel.com
www.lespressesdureel.com

Germany and Austria
Vice Versa Vertrieb, Immanuelkirchstrasse 12, D-10405 Berlin
info@vice-versa-vertrieb.de
www.vice-versa-vertrieb.de

UK and other European countries
Cornerhouse Publications, 70 Oxford Street, UK-Manchester M1 5NH
publications@cornerhouse.org
www.cornerhouse.org/books

USA, Canada, Asia, and Australia
ARTBOOK|D.A.P., 155 Sixth Avenue, 2nd Floor, USA-New York, NY 10013
dap@dapinc.com
www.artbook.com

For a list of our partner bookshops or for any general questions, please contact JRP|Ringier directly at info@jrp-ringier.com, or visit our homepage www.jrp-ringier.com for further information about our program.

ISBN 978-3-03764-119-4

WWW.COLLAGECULTURE.COM